PRICE ACTION
TRADING SECRETS

2021

**Trading Strategies to You Become a
Consistently Profitable Trader**

DISCLAIMER

The information contained in this book is for educational purposes only.

No representation is being made that any account will or is likely to achieve profits or losses similar to those discussed in this book. The past performance of any trading system or methodology is not necessarily indicative of future results.

By reading this book, you agree that my company and I are not responsible for the success or failure of your trading business.

The ideas I'm about to present are ones that I've learned from other traders (see the acknowledgements section) and I don't claim to be the original source of them.

TABLE OF CONTENT

INTRODUCTION

When I was 20 years old, I read a book on investing called: *Buffettology*. It explained how the world's richest investor, Warren Buffet, chose companies to invest in.

I was fascinated by how a man could become so wealthy simply by picking the right stocks to hold for the long run. Who wouldn't be?

After reading *Buffettology*, I was hooked. I began looking for anything I could find to make myself a great investor.

I read books on value investing and fundamental analysis. After a while, I noticed the authors kept repeating the same three elements:

- Ensure the company has more assets than liabilities.

- Ensure revenue, net income, and cash flow are increasing every year.

- Ensure the company has growth potential.

Et voilà: The secret to successful investing!

Now, armed with my newfound knowledge, I was ready to pounce on any opportunities that appeared on the markets.

The first stock I bought was Sembcorp Marine in 2009 because it had solid fundamentals and the markets were recovering from the financial crisis.

I went long at $3.28 and told myself to hold this stock until the price doubled!

Five days later, I bailed out at $3.08. *What a chicken I was.*

Then, after some reflection, I realized my emotions had triggered this action. So, unwilling to give up just yet, and with the markets making a bull run, I knew I had to get back in the game.

Being naive and ambitious, I did more research and bought more companies —with margin.

Here's what I bought: I went long on Noble Group, Keppel Land, and Sembcorp Marine with an initial outlay of $20,000.

In two months, I was up close to $10,000. But being a fundamentalist who was trying to emulate Warren Buffet, I held on.

At this point, I felt like a champion with a knack for picking stocks. Even my broker commented that everything I touched turned to gold.

Two weeks later, my $10,000 in unrealized profits vaporized. The euro debt crisis had hit the markets.

Now I had nothing to show but my bitterness. Eventually, I bailed out of all my positions because I couldn't bear the pain of watching my profits turned into losses.

After my failed attempt at being an investor, I figured being a trader would be better—and that's when I started trading on the forex (foreign exchange) market.

Because I was new to forex trading, I looked to the Internet for help. I browsed forums, books, and whatever I could get my hands on.

My first taste of trading came when I was learning from a "guru" (on an online forum). He had a huge following and many traders worshipped him like a god.

I figured, they can't all be wrong, can they? So I learned from him too.

He taught us to use Bollinger Bands, to buy at the lows and sell at the highs. I traded this strategy for a while and made money at the start, only to lose it all later.

Then, I came across a quote that said something like this: "Indicators are useless because they lag behind the markets. Focus on price instead."

This led me to the world of price action trading. I learned about support and resistance, trendlines, candlestick patterns, and many other things.

Again, I had a few winning trades at the start, but slowly, the losses came and eroded all my profits.

At this point, I wondered to myself, "Maybe the strategies I'm using are too simple. I need to find something more complex so the chances of it working will be higher."

This brought me to the world of harmonic patterns where I learned about stuff like the Gartley, the Crab, the Shark, the Cypher, etc. (I'm not kidding. Those were the actual names of the patterns).

Again, the results were the same and the cycle repeated itself for four-plus years.

At that point, I was frustrated and confused. I asked myself, "What the heck are the profitable traders doing that I'm not?"

After years of trial and error, I finally realized my mistake. It wasn't the strategies, the systems, or the chart patterns.

Rather, my mistakes were rooted in my lack of understanding of the natural laws of trading. I fought against these laws and paid the price. But when I finally embraced them, my trading changed forever.

Today, I manage a seven-figure portfolio, trade across forex, stocks, and ETFs, and have more than 100,000 traders following my TradingwithRayner blog each month. *What a ride!*

So you might be wondering, "If you're so good, why write a book and give away all your secrets?" That's a great question. Here's why: *There are no secrets when it comes to trading.*

If you're talking about price action trading (or discretionary trading), then there are no secrets since most of the information can be found in books, courses, and online sources.

Also, price action trading is subjective. The way you interpret a chart will naturally be different from the way another trader sees it. For example, if you asked five traders to draw support and resistance lines, you'd likely get five different answers. This means that even if something is a secret, the subjective nature of price action trading will affect the way people interpret that secret.

And this brings me to the question: If there are no secrets in price action trading, then why write a book about it? Well, there are three reasons. Here's the first one:

It will make me more money.

Here's the truth. Writing a book will make me more money and diversify my sources of income. Also, if you think my book is good, there's a good chance you'll sign up for my premium training programs in the future (and that will make me even more money).

Here's the second reason:

It will inspire my children.

I want my children to know that they can achieve anything they set their minds to. If Papa can write a book, so can I. If Papa can be a trader, so can If Papa can do it, so can I!

And here's the third:

I'll be able to leave behind a legacy.

In the end, I want to leave something behind in this world. Call it a legacy, sheer ego, or whatever. I just want to be remembered even after I'm gone. And to achieve this, I must write a damn good book so I'll be remembered— and I hope *Price Action Trading Secrets* is the kind of book that will be remembered.

There you have it! Those are the reasons why I wrote *Price Action Trading Secrets*, and I hope you get as much value out of reading it as I'm getting out of writing it. So let's kick things off!

HERE'S WHAT YOU'LL LEARN IN *PRICE ACTION TRADING SECRETS*:

- How to trade the markets without relying on fundamentals news, trading indicators, or signal services.

- How to better time your entries and exits so you can reduce your losses and maximize your profits.

- How to trade along the path of least resistance so you can improve your winning rate and increase your profit potential.

- How to identify profitable trading opportunities across different markets and time frames.

- How to manage your risk like a professional trader and never blow up another trading account.

- How to remain calm in your trading even if the market "throws surprises" at you.

- A proven framework you can use to become a consistently profitable trader (even if you have no trading experience).

- Advanced price action trading techniques that nobody tells you.

There are also bonus resources that accompany this book to enhance your learning experience. You can get them at priceactiontradingsecrets.com/bonus.

Finally, if you want to succeed in this business, never trust anything and always verify everything because no one is going to do the work for you. Cool?

Then let's roll!

THE NATURAL LAWS OF TRADING THAT NOBODY TELLS YOU

Let me ask you this: When you throw an Apple, what happens next? Well, it's only a matter of time before the Apple drops to the ground, right? That's because the law of gravity is at play here.

And it's the same with trading. Certain laws govern profitable trading, and if you break them, it's nearly impossible to become a consistently profitable trader.

So here are the natural laws of trading that you need to embrace if you want to become a profitable trader.

FOLLOWING A CONSISTENT SET OF ACTIONS LEADS TO CONSISTENT RESULTS

I know this sounds like a no-brainer, but it's true. You must follow a consistent set of actions if you want consistent results.

This is easier said than done because when you encounter a losing streak, you'll have the urge to do something about it.

You'll have thoughts like this:

"Let me remove my stop loss so I don't get stopped out."

"Let me double down so I can recoup my losses quickly."

"This strategy is not working anymore, let me find something else."

And if you give in to your thoughts, you won't be consistent in your strategy —which means you won't get consistent results.

The bottom line is this: If you want to become a consistent trader, you must have a consistent set of actions.

YOU MUST HAVE AN EDGE

IN THE MARKETS

Now, even if you are consistent in your actions, this doesn't mean you'll be a consistently profitable trader. Why?

Because your trading strategy must provide you with an edge in the markets. What do I mean by having an edge?

Let me give you an example:

Let's say I make a bet with you. Every time you toss a coin, and it comes up heads, you win $2. And if it comes up tails, you lose $1.

In the long run, you'll make money with this arrangement because you have an edge over me.

And it's the same with trading. If you want to profit from the markets in the long run, your trading strategy must give you an edge.

This is because without an edge, even if you have the best risk management, discipline, and psychology, you'll still be a losing trader.

THE LAW OF LARGE NUMBERS

This is an important concept to grasp. The law of large number states that in the short run, your results are random, but they'll align towards its expectancy in the long run.

I know that sounds confusing so let me give you an example.

Let's say you toss a coin 10 times and you get 6 heads and 4 tails. Would you claim the coin has a 60% chance of coming up heads and a 40% chance of coming up tails? Of course not.

Intuitively, you understand this because you only tossed the coin 10 times. But if you were to toss the coin 1000 times, it would be closer to 50% heads and 50% tails.

And this is what the law of large numbers is about. In the short run, your trading results are random. And it's only in the long run, after a decent sample size of trades, that your system will align toward its expectancy.

This is important to understand because if you're unaware of it, you'll abandon your trading strategy after a few losing trades without understanding that the results you've been observing are actually random.

ALWAYS TAKE CARE OF YOUR DOWNSIDE

The most important rule of trading is to play great defense, not great offence. — Paul Tudor Jones.

Here's the thing: Your trading strategy can have an edge in the markets, but without proper risk management, you'll still blow up your trading account.

Let me give you an example.

Imagine there are two traders, John and Sally.

John is an aggressive trader, and he risks 25% of his account on each trade.

Sally is a conservative trader, and she risks 1% of her account on each trade.

Both adopt a trading strategy that wins 50% of the time with an average risk-to-reward ratio of 1:2.

Over the next 8 trades, the outcomes are lose, lose, lose, lose, win, win, win, win.

Before you think this is an unlikely scenario, remember the law of large numbers?

So here's the outcome for John:

$$-25\% \; -25\% \; -25\% \; -25\% = \text{BLOW UP}$$

Here's the outcome for Sally:

$$-1\% \; -1\% \; -1\% \; -1\% \; +2\% \; +2\% \; +2\% \; +2\% = +4\%$$

Are you getting the hang of how important this is?

Risk management can be a deciding factor in whether you're a consistently profitable trader or a losing trader.

Remember, you can have the best trading strategy in the world. But without proper risk management, you will still blow up your trading account. It's not a question of if, but when.

YOU NEED MONEY TO MAKE MONEY

Sorry to burst your bubble, but you need money to make money in this business. Here's why.

Let's say you make an average of 20%/year.

- On a $1,000 account, you'll make $200/year.

- On a $100,000 account, you'll make $20,000/year.

- On a $1M account, you'll make $200,000/year.

Now, you might think that 20% a year is too low and that you can make 100% a year.

Sure, that's possible by taking huge risks. But I'm talking about making consistent returns, not "go-big-or-go-home" kinds of returns.

Don't believe me? Then ask yourself, why do hedge funds raise millions (or even billions) of dollars? Why don't they just trade their own money without having anyone to answer to? It's because they want you to be rich and make this world a better place. Hmm.

YOU MAKE BIG MONEY BY COMPOUNDING YOUR RETURNS

Sure, you can make a living trading full-time. But if you want to make big money, then you must compound your returns. Let me give you an example.

Let's say you make an average of 20% a year with a $100,000 account. Every year, you use all your trading profits to sustain your lifestyle. This means you're back at $100,000 at the start of the next year. But what if you have a job or business that covers your expenses so you don't have to withdraw money from your account. How would this change things? Let's use my example again.

You make an average of 20% a year on a $100,000 account, but if you don't withdraw your profits, you can compound your returns over time. After 10 years, your account will be worth $619,173. After 20 years, it will be worth $3,833,759. After 30 years, it will be worth $23,737,631. You get my point.

But do you know where the biggest money is made? Other people's money (OPM). Yup, you read me right. The biggest money is made by managing other people's money. But don't take my word for it. Just look at the richest finance people on *Forbes*, and you'll see that most of them own hedge funds. And what do hedge funds do? They manage other people's money.

THERE'S NO BEST TRADING STRATEGY OUT THERE

This is one of the most common questions I get from traders: "Hey Rayner, what is the best trading strategy out there?"

I'll be honest. There's no such thing as the best trading strategy because it's not possible to define what "best" means. "Best" could mean many things: highest returns, lowest drawdown, least time required, low capital requirements, the list goes on. Clearly, what's "best" to you might seem terrible to someone else.

So instead of looking for the best trading strategy, you first have to know what your trading goals are. Once you understand that, you can select the "best" trading strategy to meet your goals.

NO TRADING STRATEGY WORKS ALL THE TIME

Trading strategies seek to exploit certain "patterns" in the markets. If you want a trading strategy to work all the time, market conditions must remain the same.

But ask yourself, is this possible? If you've traded long enough, you'll know it's not because the market is always changing. It can move from an uptrend to a downtrend, low volatility to high volatility, and so on.

And if the markets are always changing, then it means no trading strategy works all the time (and this is how a drawdown occurs).

So forget about using a single trading strategy to make money every day (or every week). It doesn't work that way.

Instead, you'll go through a cycle of *ups and downs*. You want to keep your profits during the good times so you can pay for your losses during the bad. The key is to play good defense so you can survive to experience the good times again.

THE SECRET TO MAKING PROFITS EVERY DAY

This is the secret to making daily profits: The frequency of your trades. Yes, you read me right. If you want to make money every single day, you need to trade frequently so the law of large numbers can work in your favor (within a short time frame).

Confused? No worries, I'll explain. Imagine the following scenario:

- You have a special coin in your hands.
- If it comes up heads, you win $2.
- If it comes up tails, you lose $1.

But here's the catch: You can only toss your coin once a day. Do you think you'll be able to make money every single day doing this?

Of course not. Why? Because in the short run, your coin toss results are random—you could get tails many times in a row (and thus lose many days in a row).

Now, what if you could toss your coin 1,000 times a day? How would the results change? Well, you'd get close to 50% heads and 50% tails after 1,000 tosses—which means you'd be guaranteed to make money every day because your edge could play out within a short period of time.

Does this make sense? Great! Because this concept is the same as trading. If you want to make money every day, you must have a high frequency of trades.

But is this feasible for a retail trader? In my opinion, the odds are stacked against you because commissions are sky high, and it's unlikely you'll be able to (consistently and profitably) spot a sufficiently high number of trading opportunities with your naked eye alone.

That's why this field is largely dominated by high-frequency trading firms, and yes, they can make money (almost) every day. One example is Virtu Financial, which according to *Bloomberg*, had one day of trading losses in 1,238 days (during the 2009–2014 period).

So does this mean you can't trade for a living? Nope, it doesn't mean that. It means you shouldn't expect to make money every single day—and this isn't to say that you can't make money every quarter or every year.

TRADING IS A GET-RICH-SLOW SCHEME

Many people get involved in trading because they want to make money—and they want to make it fast. But I'm here to tell you trading is a get-rich-slow scheme.

Sure, you can make money fast, but you'll lose it equally as fast (or faster). So if you want longevity in your career, treat trading as a business (not a get-rich-quick scheme).

Here's how it works:

If you start with a $5,000 account, and you make an average of 20% a year, after 20 years, your account will be worth $191,688.

But let's take things a step further. Let's add another $5,000 to your account every year. Again, if you make an average of 20% a year, after 20 years, it'll be worth $1,311,816.

How "fast" you can get rich depends on two things: your account size and your percentage return. Sure, you can increase your return by risking more, but the risk of drawdown is larger—and you risk losing everything.

So my suggestion is to risk small, add more funds regularly, and compound your way to riches. Yes, it takes time, but the risk of ruin is dramatically reduced.

AT THIS POINT...

You've learned the natural laws of trading and how they work. This will give you a good idea of what profitable trading is about so you can ignore the noise and focus on the stuff that matters.

Next, we'll look at the basics of price action trading. You'll learn what it is, why it matters, and what its pros and cons are.

SUMMARY

- If you want to be a consistent trader, you must be consistent in your actions.

- You must have an edge in the markets because without one, even the best risk management or trading psychology won't save your account.

- The law of large numbers means your trading results will be random in the short run. In the long run, they'll align towards its expectancy.

- Always take care of your downside. The best trading strategy is useless if you don't contain your losses.

- You need money to make money in this business.

- The big money is made from compounding your returns, and the biggest money is made from managing other people's money (OPM).

- There's no such thing as the best trading strategy because "best" is subjective.

- No trading strategy works all the time because the markets are always changing.

- Trading frequency matters. Don't expect to make money every day if you only take two trades per day.

- Trading is a get-rich-slow scheme. If you add funds to your account regularly and compound them over time, you'll eventually get rich—but it takes time.

WHAT IS PRICE ACTION TRADING AND HOW DOES IT WORK?

Here's the deal: Most traders think the price goes up because there are more buyers than sellers. Nope. Here's why.

Let's say there are 100 buyers, each wanting to buy one share of Google. At the same time, there's one seller, but the seller wants to sell one million shares of Google.

What do you think would happen to the price? Would it go up or down? It'll go down because the selling pressure is greater than the buying pressure.

This has nothing to do with there being more buyers than sellers because, in this case, there are more buyers than sellers. But the price is still going down because the selling pressure is greater.

And this is what price action trading is about: Understanding the imbalance between buying and selling pressure so you can better time your entries and exits—and improve your trading results.

So what are the benefits of price action trading?

- You can ignore fundamental news because price is all you need.
- Unlike trading indicators, the price is the price.
- You can better time your entries and exits.
- You have a framework to trade in different market conditions.

Let me explain this further.

YOU CAN IGNORE FUNDAMENTAL NEWS BECAUSE PRICE IS ALL YOU NEED

Now, you might be thinking, "But Rayner, fundamentals are what drive the market. How can I ignore them?"

Let me ask you, have you ever noticed how the market goes down when there's bad news and up when there's good news?

Here's an example:

AMD stock had negative earnings in 2014, 2015, and 2016. But the stock price still gained 700% in 12 months.

Figure 1.1 – AMD share price up 700% in 12 months despite negative earnings (AMD Daily)

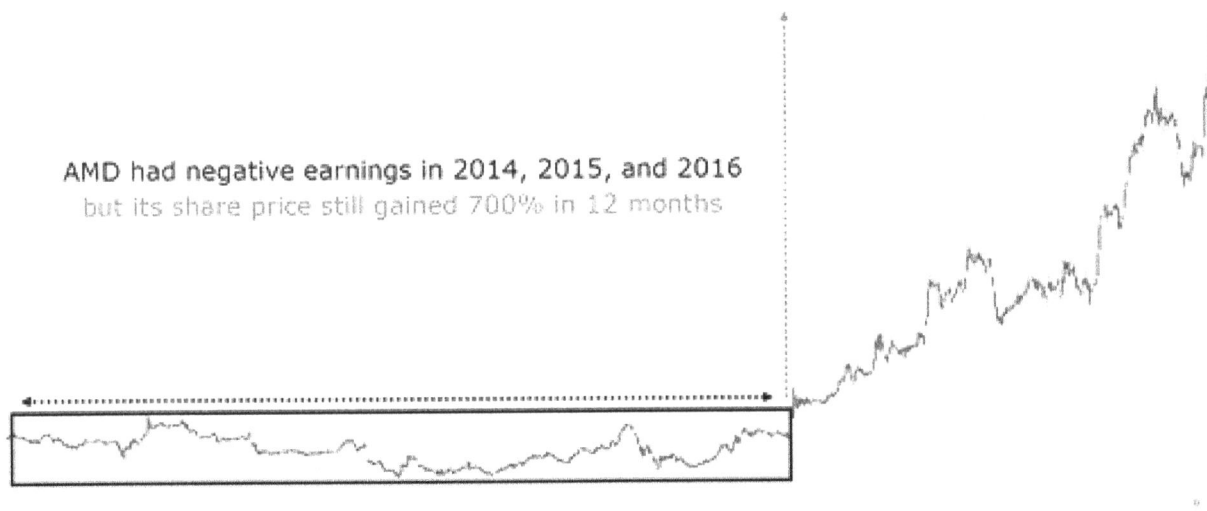

If you were trading based on the news, you probably got burned and missed the monster rally.

But what if you ignored the news and just followed price? How would that turn out?

Since we're on this topic, let me tell you a secret.

Have you ever wondered how financial news always have a reason for the market ups and downs?

It's because they have a slew of positive and negative news on standby. If the market is up, they choose to share the positive news. And if it's down, they focus on the negative news.

That's why there's always positive and negative fundamental news floating around. And the type of news that's shared is dictated by the price movement, not the other way around.

Have you ever heard a news reporter say, "I have no idea why the market went down today."

Nope, it never happens. They always know the cause because they have a list of "reasons" to choose from.

THE PRICE GIVES YOU AN OBJECTIVE VIEW OF THE MARKETS (WITHOUT MANIPULATION)

Most trading indicators work by applying a formula to the price. For example, a 200-day moving average calculates the average closing price over the last 200 days.

Now, there's nothing wrong with using indicators in your trading, provided you understand how they work.

But if you don't, you'll be manipulated by trading indicators.

Let me give you an example. The relative strength index (RSI) indicator shows oversold on the daily timeframe. But if you "adjust" the settings, you can change the RSI to overbought.

That's because the RSI calculates the average gains to losses over a fixed number of periods. And if you adjust the number of periods, you'll get a different RSI reading.

So which settings do you trust? The overbought or the oversold RSI? And there lies the problem. If you're not careful, you can manipulate indicators to fit your bias (and that's a recipe for disaster).

Now, what about price action? Well, the price is the price – and what you see is what you get. No formulas, no "adjustment," and less manipulation.

(I say less manipulation because in less liquid markets, the price can still be manipulated by those with deeper pockets).

YOU CAN BETTER TIME YOUR ENTRIES AND EXITS

As you know, trading indicators work by applying mathematical formulas to the price. So they're slower to react, and that's how you get the saying "indicators lag behind the market."

This means when you use price action to time your entries and exits, you'll be faster than someone who relies on indicators.

But remember, just because indicators lag, doesn't mean they're useless because they're a great tool to filter your trading setups, trade management, etc.

Now, it's beyond the scope of this book to discuss indicators. But if you want to learn more, then download the PATS bonus resource, where you'll learn how to use indicators effectively. Here's the link: priceactiontradingsecrets.com/bonus

YOU HAVE A FRAMEWORK TO TRADE IN DIFFERENT MARKET CONDITIONS

Imagine you wanted to build a house. Would you randomly install the doors, toilet bowls, bathrooms, and bedrooms whenever you felt like it?

Of course not. You'd have a framework (or blueprint) so you'd know the layout and design of your house. Only then, would you execute the work on your house.

It's the same for trading. You don't just blindly place buy and sell orders whenever you feel like it. You must have a framework for trading the markets that includes a plan for when to buy, when to sell, and when to stay out of the markets.

That's how price action trading comes into play because it helps you to identify the different market conditions so you can use the appropriate trading strategy to respond to them. And when the market changes, so should your trading strategy.

At this point, you're all excited about mastering price action trading. But wait. Before you begin, I want to share the downsides of price action trading with you so that you're aware of them:

- It's near impossible to perform an accurate backtest.

- It takes a lot of time to validate a trading strategy.

- There's subjectivity involved.

Let me discuss these points in more detail.

IT'S NEAR IMPOSSIBLE TO PERFORM AN ACCURATE BACKTEST

When you backtest discretionary trading strategies, you're looking at historical data and "pretending" that you're trading live.

You scroll through the charts until you're looking at the earliest possible date, and you unfold each bar one by one, simulating what would happen as if it's occurring in real-time.

Then, you decide whether you'll enter or exit your trades according to your strategy—and record the performance over the backtest period.

Now, the problem with this approach is that your bias will skew your results.

For example, if you see that bitcoin is in an uptrend from 2015 to 2017, your bias will be on the long side (and you'll avoid shorting).

In addition, you'll be more likely to make errors in recording the result of each trade, which will make the results less reliable.

IT TAKES A LOT OF TIME TO VALIDATE A TRADING STRATEGY

The alternative to backtesting is forward testing. Instead of looking at past data, you trade live and see how your trading strategy performs in real-time. If you're a short-term trader, you'll be able to get a decent sample size of trades within a few months.

However, for long-term traders, this may take a year or two. If you're going down this path, it makes sense to have a full-time job and do this part-time so you reduce your opportunity cost.

THERE'S SUBJECTIVITY INVOLVED

Price action trading falls under discretionary trading. And when you trade in this manner, there's subjectivity involved.

For example, if you ask two traders to identify patterns on a chart, you'll get two different answers. Why? It's because they each have their own interpretation of the market based on their own experiences and biases.

That's why as a price action trader, it's important to have a framework you can use to minimize subjectivity (and that's what this book is all about).

Now, you can't avoid subjectivity entirely. But it is something you'll want to minimize as much as you can in order to be consistent in your trading.

AT THIS POINT…

You've learned what price action trading is about, why it matters, and what its pros and cons are.

In the next chapter, we'll dive into the first component of price action trading: market structure. You'll discover how the market really moves, so you'll be able to gauge whether to buy, sell, or stay out of the markets. Let's go!

SUMMARY

- Price action trading is about understanding the imbalance between buying and selling pressure so that you can identify trading opportunities and make a profit.

- As a price action trader, price is king—everything else is secondary.

- Price action trading is not a strategy but a framework for trading in different market conditions.

- Price action trading is not the holy grail, and it has its downsides. For instance, it's impossible to perform an accurate backtest, it takes a lot of time to validate a trading strategy, and there is subjectivity is involved.

MARKET STRUCTURE: DECODING THE SECRET BEHAVIOR OF THE MARKETS

When I started trading, I always wondered if there was a secret pattern that the smart money knew that I didn't. Otherwise, how could you explain a sudden collapse in the price when the market was looking bullish (or a sudden rally when the market looked "dead")?

Then, I studied the works of Richard Wyckoff and Stan Weinstein. That's when things finally made sense. You see, the market doesn't go up and down in a straight line. There's an ebb and flow to it.

If you pay close attention, you'll realize the market moves in stages: accumulation, advancing, distribution, and declining. This means if you know what stage the market is at, you'll never have to second guess whether you should be buying or selling. Everything becomes clear, as if you have X-ray vision for seeing what the market is really doing. Sound awesome? Then let's get started.

1. ACCUMULATION STAGE

An accumulation stage occurs after a decline in price, and it looks like a range market within a downtrend. The logic behind this is the market can only go so low before the buyers step in and push the price higher.

When that happens, you've got traders selling in the downtrend and traders buying at "cheap" prices. When these two forces collide, the market goes into an equilibrium, otherwise known as an accumulation stage.

Now, it's called an accumulation stage because this is where the smart money accumulates their position in anticipation of higher prices to come.

Here are the characteristics of an accumulation stage:

- It occurs after the price has fallen over the last five months or more (on the daily timeframe).

- It looks like a range market with obvious areas of support and resistance within a downtrend.

- The 200-day moving average starts to flatten out.

- The price swings back and forth around the 200-day moving average.

Here's an example of an accumulation stage:

Figure 2.1 – Accumulation stage (Wheat Daily)

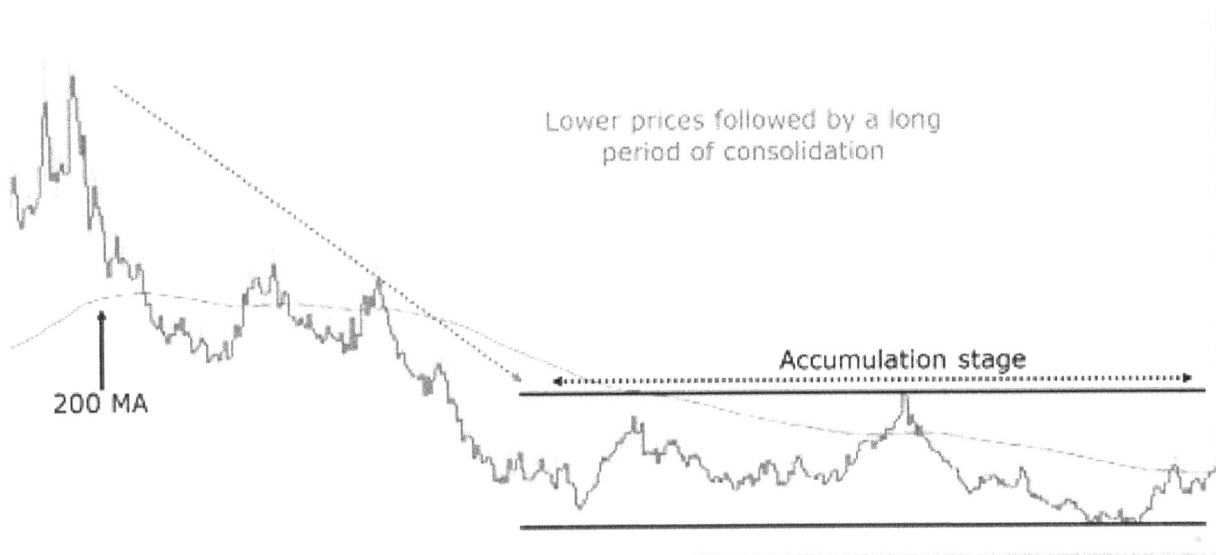

Now, this is important. Just because the market is in an accumulation stage doesn't mean it will break out higher. It can also break down. And if that happens, the downtrend resumes (remember, trading is about probabilities, never certainties).

But if the market breaks out of resistance, that's where we move onto the next stage.

2. ADVANCING STAGE

The advancing stage occurs when the price breaks out of resistance (from the accumulation stage), which is otherwise known as an uptrend. This happens because the market can't remain in a range forever. Eventually, one side of the market will dominate and that's the start of a new uptrend (or the resumption of the downtrend).

So for an advancing stage to occur, the buying pressure must overcome the selling pressure, which leads to the start of a new uptrend.

Here are the characteristics of an advancing stage:

- It occurs after the price breaks out of resistance in an accumulation stage.

- You'll see a series of higher highs and lows.

- The price is above the 200-day moving average.

- The 200-day moving average is starting to point higher.

Here's what I mean:

Figure 2.2 – Advancing stage (Bund Daily)

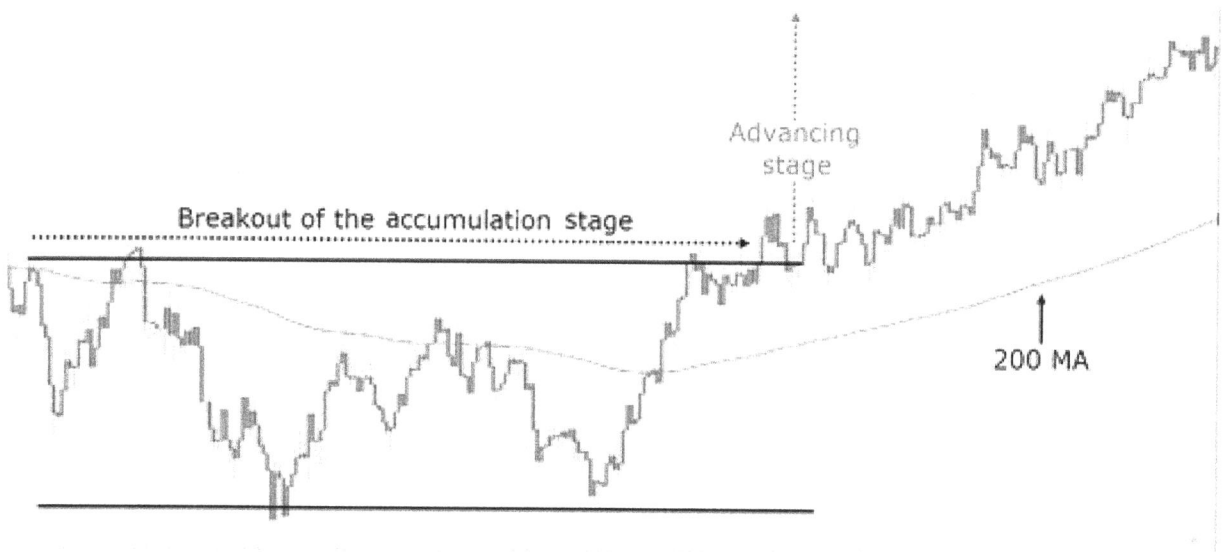

3. DISTRIBUTION STAGE

A distribution stage occurs after an advance in price, and it looks like a range market within an uptrend. The logic behind this is that the market can only go so high before the sellers come and short the markets.

When this happens, you've got traders buying in an uptrend and traders shorting at "high" prices. When these two forces collide, the market goes into an equilibrium, otherwise known as the distribution stage.

At this point, it's called a distribution stage because this is where the smart money distributes away their position in anticipation of lower prices to come.

Here are the characteristics of a distribution stage:

- It occurs after the price has risen for the last five months or more (on the daily timeframe).

- It looks like a range market with obvious support and resistance areas in an uptrend.

- The 200-day moving average starts to flatten out.

- The price whips back and forth around the 200-day moving average.

It looks something like this:

Figure 2.3 – Distribution stage (GBP/USD Daily)

At this point, there's no guarantee the market will break down. But if it breaks below support, that's where we move on to the final stage.

4. DECLINING STAGE

The declining stage occurs when the price breaks down of support (from the distribution stage), otherwise known as a downtrend. This is because the market can't remain in a range forever. Eventually, one side of the market will dominate, and that's either the start of a new downtrend (or the resumption of the uptrend).

So for a declining stage to occur, the selling pressure must overcome the buying pressure, which leads to the start of a new downtrend.

Here are the characteristics of a declining stage:

- It occurs after the price breaks out of support in a distribution stage.
- You'll see a series of lower highs and lows.
- The price is below the 200-day moving average.
- The 200-day moving average is starting to point lower.

Here's an example:

Figure 2.4 – Declining stage (Brent Crude Oil Daily)

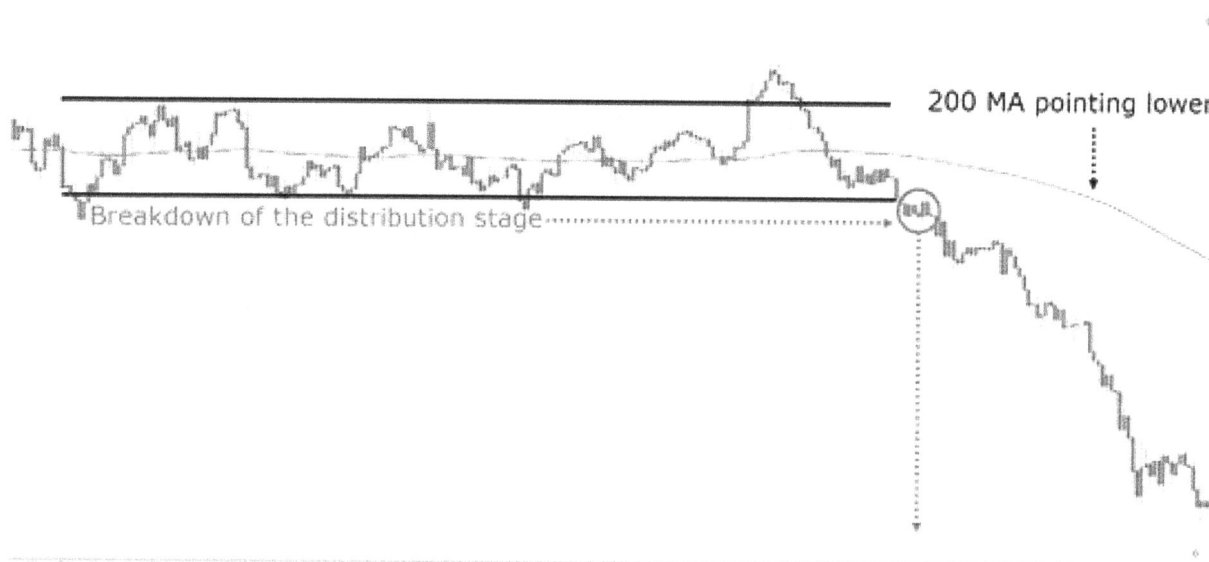

200 MA pointing lower

Breakdown of the distribution stage

Now you might be thinking, "What's the point of learning these four stages of the market?" It's this: If you can identify which stage the market is in, you'll know whether to be a buyer or seller.

For example, if the market is in a potential accumulation stage, then you know there's a huge potential upside if the price breaks above resistance, so you'll want to look for buying opportunities. Perhaps near the lows of support, the breakout of resistance, or the first pullback after the breakout, etc.

And if the market is in a declining stage? Then you'll want to look for shorting opportunities, possibly towards an area of value like resistance, a moving average, etc. Can you see how useful this is?

Okay, I'll be honest. There will be times when the market structure isn't obvious. So what do you do in this scenario? You stay out of that market. There are plenty of trading opportunities with "cleaner" market structure. So don't force a trade if you don't have a read on the markets.

AT THIS POINT...

You've learned about market structure and you understand how the market really moves (with the help of the concepts from the four stages).

This means you know what to do in different market conditions, whether to buy, sell, or stay out of the markets.

However, market structure doesn't tell you where to enter or exit your trades. I've saved that for the next chapter, so read on.

SUMMARY

- An accumulation stage occurs after a decline in price, and it looks like a range market within a downtrend.

- The advancing stage occurs when the price breaks out of resistance (from the accumulation stage), otherwise known as an uptrend.

- A distribution stage occurs after an advance in price, and it looks like a range market within an uptrend.

- The declining stage occurs when the price breaks down of support (from the distribution stage), otherwise known as a downtrend.

THE TRUTH ABOUT SUPPORT AND RESISTANCE

Eleven years at school, two years at college, three years at university, and all I needed to do was learn how to draw a horizontal line — Tom Dante.

I couldn't help but laugh when I first read that quote. It sounds silly, but that's how much support and resistance matter to price action (or discretionary) traders.

So in this chapter, you'll learn about support and resistance: How to draw it, the truth that nobody tells you about, and how to tell when support and resistance will break.

WHAT ARE SUPPORT AND RESISTANCE, AND HOW DO THEY WORK?

Support: the horizontal area on your charts where potential buying pressure could come in and push the price higher.

Resistance: the horizontal area on your charts where selling pressure could come in and push the price lower.

In short, you can treat support and resistance as areas of value on your charts to help you buy low and sell high.

Here's an example of support:

Figure 3.1 – Support (USD/CAD Daily)

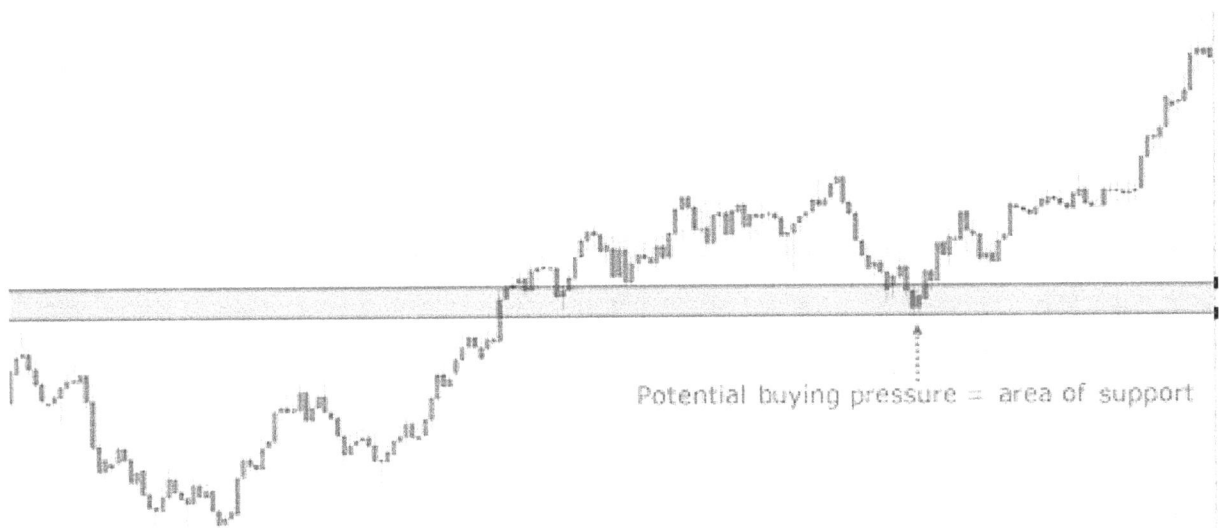

Potential buying pressure = area of support

Here's an example of resistance:

Figure 3.2 – Resistance (GBP/JPY Daily)

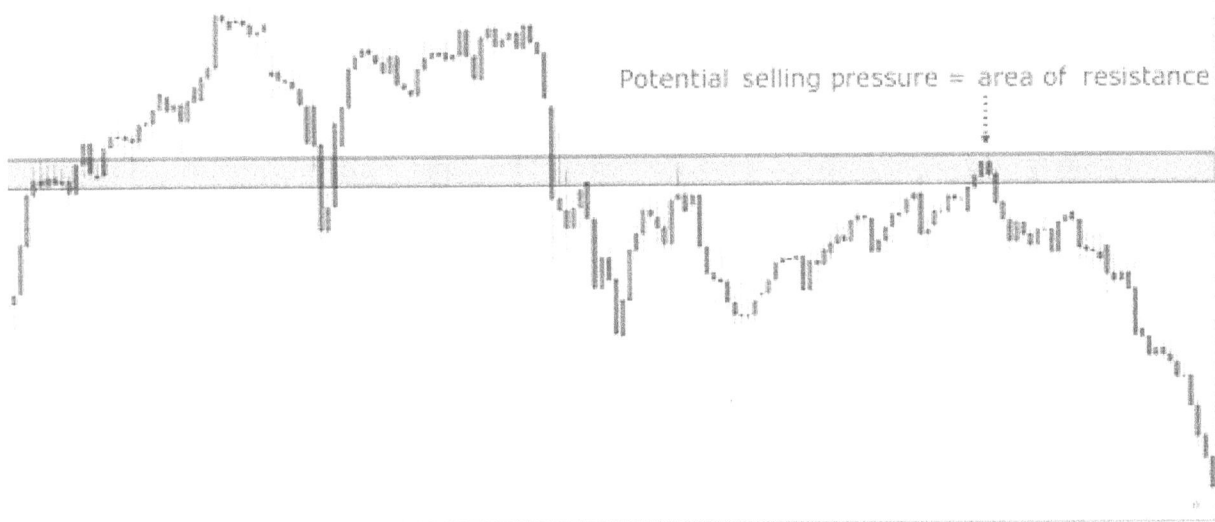

Potential selling pressure = area of resistance

Now the question is, how do you draw support and resistance? As you already know, this is subjective, and there are many ways of doing it.

So here are some guidelines I use when drawing support and resistance:

1. Zoom your charts out so they show at least 300 candles.

2. Draw the most obvious levels (if you need to second guess yourself, it probably isn't worth drawing).

3. Adjust the levels to get as many "touches" as possible.

Here are a couple of examples:

Figure 3.3 – Have at least 300 candles on your chart when drawing support and resistance (CHF/JPY Daily)

At least 300 candles

−0.339 (−0.30%), −33.9
312 bars, 442d

Figure 3.4 – Identify the most obvious levels that stick out in your face (CHF/JPY Daily)

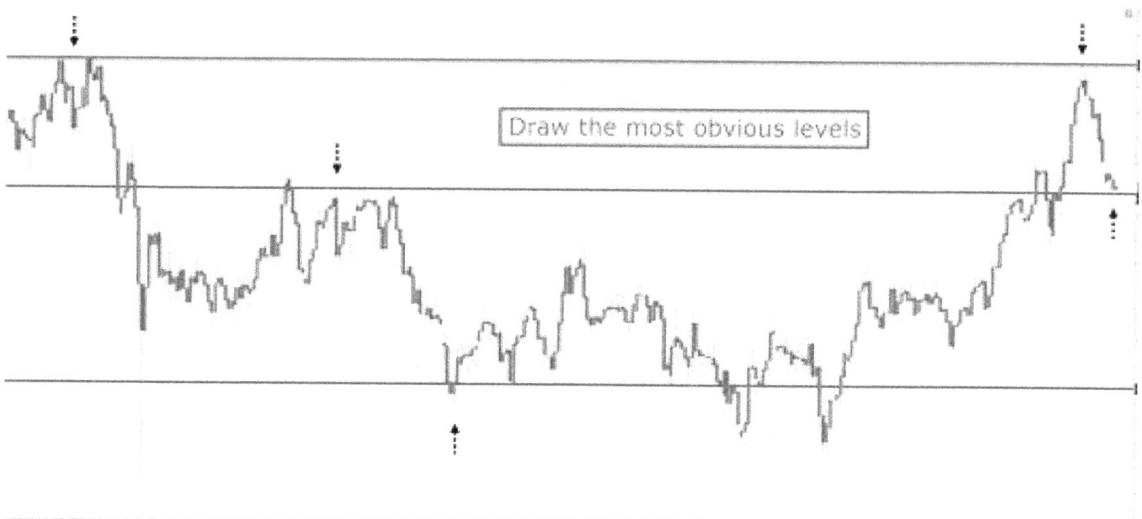

Draw the most obvious levels

Clearly, it's difficult to explain how to draw support and resistance in a book. That's why I've created a training video to teach you how to do it step by step. You can access this training along with other bonus resources here: priceactiontradingsecrets.com/bonus

Next, let me share with you some concepts about support and resistance that many traders get wrong.

THE MORE TIMES SUPPORT OR RESISTANCE ARE TESTED

IN A SHORT PERIOD OF TIME, THE WEAKER THEY BECOME

I know this goes against what most trading books teach, but just because something is printed in ink, doesn't mean it's correct. Never trust anything and always validate everything, remember?

So here's my reasoning for telling you this. The market reverses at support because there's buying pressure to push the price higher. This buying pressure could be from institutions, hedge funds, or banks that have orders to fill around certain price levels.

And when the price re-tests support, some of these orders get filled. So the more the price re-tests support, the more orders get filled. And when all the orders get filled, who's left to buy?

No one, and that's when the market breaks down. Here's what I mean:

Figure 3.5 – Multiple tests of support before breakdown (USD/CAD Daily)

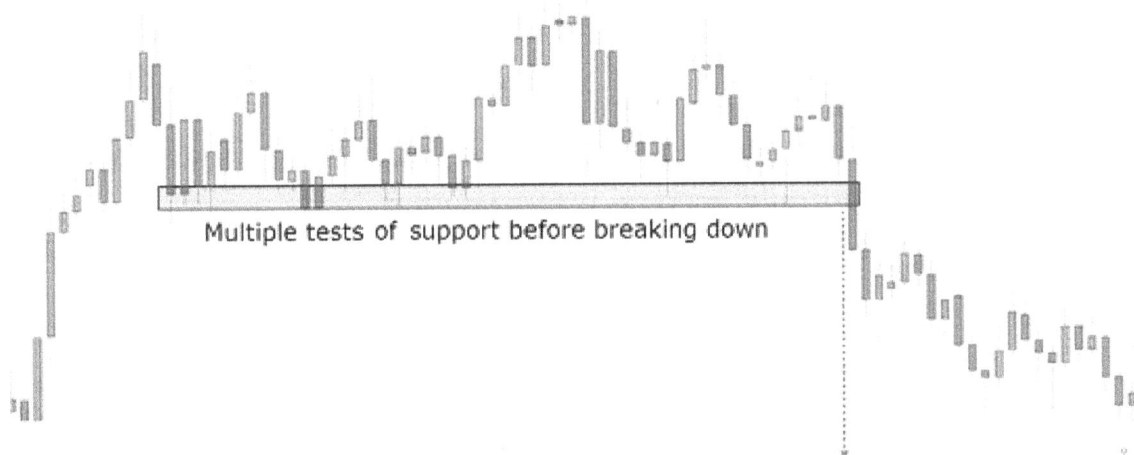

Multiple tests of support before breaking down

SUPPORT AND RESISTANCE ARE AREAS ON YOUR CHART

You might be wondering, "If support and resistance are horizontal areas, why do you draw them as lines?"

I do this because it makes my charts look cleaner and less cluttered, but I treat them as areas on my chart.

"So why is this an area on your chart and not a line?"

This is a result of two groups of traders: traders with the fear of missing out (FOMOs) and traders who want to trade at the best possible price (cheapos). Let me explain.

FOMO traders enter a trade the moment price comes to support because they're afraid of missing the move. And if there's enough buying pressure, the price will barely touch support before rallying higher.

On the other hand, cheapo traders only want to trade at the best possible price, and they look to buy at the lows of support. If there are enough traders who behave in this manner, the price will reverse near the lows of support.

But here's the thing: You have no idea which group of traders are dominant at any one time and whether what you're seeing is due to the FOMOs or the cheapos. That's why you want to treat support and resistance as an area on your charts and go in with the expectation that the market could reverse anywhere within the area. Make sense?

WHEN THE PRICE BREAKS SUPPORT, IT COULD BECOME RESISTANCE

When the price breaks below support, that horizontal area could become future resistance. And when the price breaks above resistance, that horizontal area could become future support.

Here's what it looks like:

Figure 3.6 – When the price breaks below support, it could become resistance (GBP/AUD 4-hour)

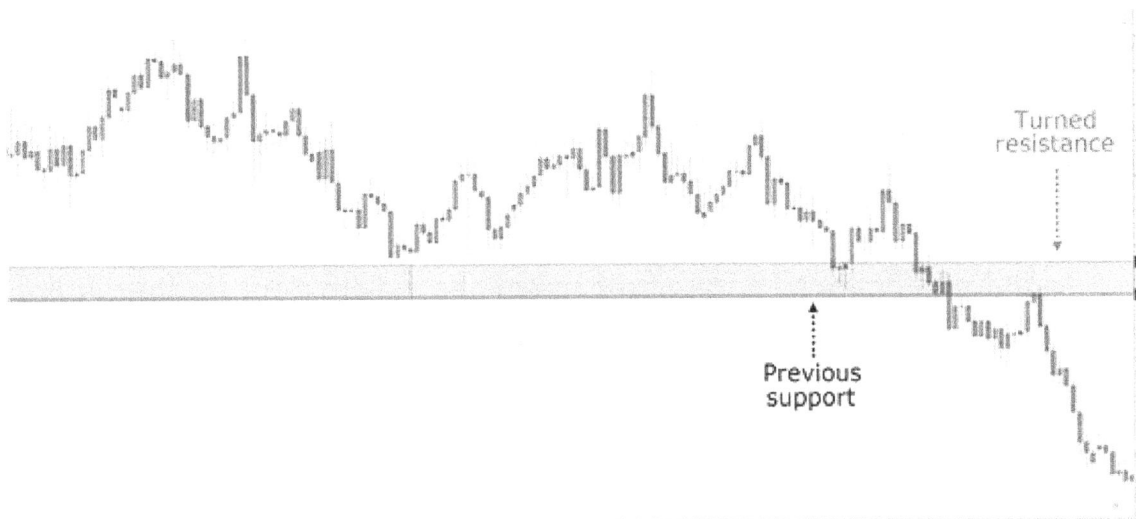

Turned resistance

Previous support

But why does this happen? Here are a few theories to explain it.

Losing traders want to exit their trade at breakeven

Imagine you bought at support thinking the price would rally higher. The next thing you know, the price collapses and you're in the red. So, you hope for a rebound to occur so you can exit your trade at breakeven (and there's no win or loss on the trade). This behavior creates selling pressure at the previous support area. And if there's enough selling pressure, the price could reverse at the previous support area, which now becomes resistance.

Traders who missed the breakout move

Sometimes the market breaks out so unexpectedly that you miss the move. And you regret your inaction, wishing you had paid more attention to the markets. So what do you do to "tame" that regret? You place a limit order at the breakout price point. If the market ever re-tests the level, you won't let it get away this time round. For example, if the price breaks out of resistance and traders miss the move, they'll place a buy limit order at the previous area of resistance (the breakout point). And if there's enough buying pressure, the price could reverse at the previous resistance area that has now become support.

Self-fulfilling prophecy

Here's how it works: If enough traders observed a phenomenon and behave in a similar manner, this phenomenon will become true. For example, if the price breaks below support and most traders expect this area of support to act as resistance, then guess what? If there's enough selling pressure, then this previous area of support now becomes resistance.

But a word of warning: Don't use the self-fulfilling prophecy as an excuse to apply all sorts of technical analysis to your trading. It doesn't work that way. Because if you're going to use something that no one's ever heard of, you're likely the only one fulfilling the prophecy. In my opinion, stick to the most popular concepts of technical analysis, because most traders will adopt them one way or another. And when they're "trapped" by using these tools, that's where you can exploit the situation to your advantage (but more on that later).

THERE ARE OTHER WAYS TO IDENTIFY AREAS OF VALUE (NOT JUST SUPPORT AND RESISTANCE)

You've learned support and resistance are horizontal areas on your chart with potential buying/selling pressure lurking nearby. However, this isn't the only way to identify areas of value on your chart.

You can also use tools like moving averages, trendlines, channels, and so on to help you identify areas of value.

For example, in a healthy trend (more on this later), the price tends to respect the 50-period moving average and this acts as an area of value. Here's what I mean:

Figure 3.7 – The price respecting the 50-period moving average (Bund Daily)

Price respecting the 50-period moving average

50 MA

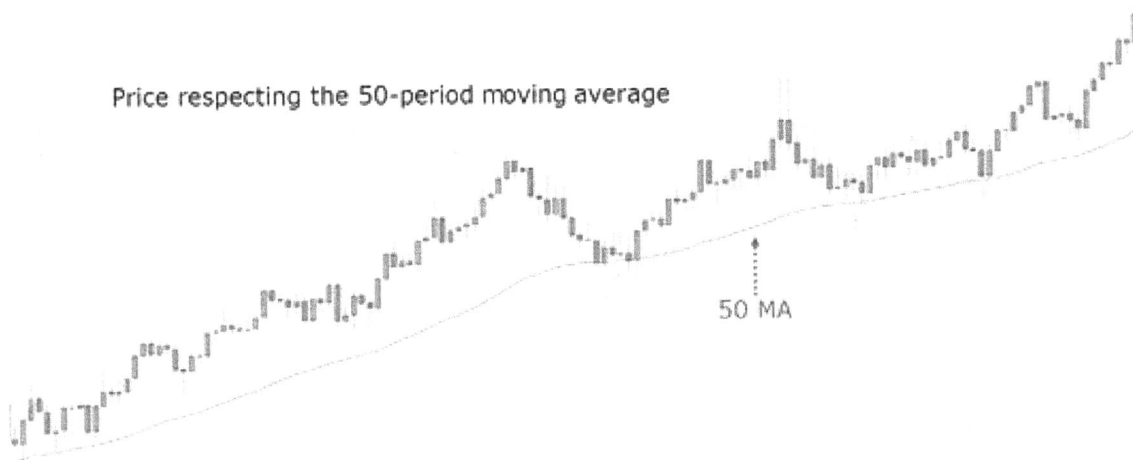

Alternatively, the market can also respect trendlines. Here's an example:

Figure 3.8 – The price respecting the trendline (Brent Crude Oil 4-hour)

Trendline acting as an area of resistance

Whatever technique you use, the concepts I shared earlier still apply. You're always dealing with an area on your charts, not a line. And the more times the market re-tests an area within a short period of time, the greater the likelihood it'll break.

HOW TO TELL WHEN SUPPORT AND RESISTANCE WILL BREAK

There's no way to tell for sure whether support or resistance will break. But here are a few things you'll want to pay attention to:

Resistance tends to break in an uptrend — As you know, an uptrend consists of higher highs and lows. And for it to continue, the price must break out of resistance (or swing high).

Support tends to break in a downtrend — Likewise, a downtrend consists of lower highs and lows. And for a downtrend to continue, the price must break out of support (or swing low).

Higher lows into resistance are a sign of strength — This looks something like an ascending triangle. It's a sign of strength because it tells you buyers are willing to buy at higher prices (despite the price being near resistance). Here's an example:

Figure 3.9 – Higher lows into resistance (GBP/USD Daily)

Lower highs into support are a sign of weakness — This looks like a descending triangle. It's a sign of weakness because it tells you sellers are willing to sell at lower prices (despite the price being near support). Here's what I mean:

Figure 3.10 – Lower highs into support (Palladium Weekly)

AT THIS POINT…

You've learned the truth about support and resistance, how they work, and how to tell when they'll break. In essence, support and resistance tell you where to buy and sell, but they don't tell you when. Don't worry, I'll cover that in the next chapter.

SUMMARY

- Support is a horizontal area on your chart where potential buying pressure could come in and push the price higher.

- Resistance is a horizontal area on your charts where selling pressure could come in and push the price lower.

- The more times support or resistance is tested within a short period of time, the greater the likelihood it will break.

- Observing support and resistance is one way to identify an area of value on your charts. Others include looking at the moving average, trendline, channel, etc.

- Support tends to break in a downtrend or when there are lower highs into support.

- Resistance tends to break in an uptrend or when there are higher lows into resistance.

3.

HOW TO MASTER CANDLESTICK PATTERNS LIKE A PRO

Back in my army days was when I was first learning about the financial markets, I had a lot of free time, and I didn't want to waste it playing "Monster Hunter," so I studied books that seemed interesting to me.

At that time, I was reading stuff on value investing, financial markets, fundamental analysis, etc. However, things took a turn when one day, my army buddy was reading a book called *Japanese Candlestick Charting Techniques* by Steve Nison.

Wow, what a game changer! It went against everything I've learned about speculation and the markets. And because it's more "appealing" than reading numbers and ratios, I was hooked! I started memorizing every single candlestick pattern in the book. You know, stuff like the hammer, the shooting star, three black crows, harami, the bullish engulfing pattern, and so on. Eventually, I got burned out trying to cram all these patterns into my head. And the worst thing was, I still couldn't make profits from any of them.

So in this chapter, you'll learn all about candlestick patterns, what they are, how they work, some information on reversal candlestick patterns, and why you don't need to memorize a single pattern (if you follow what I'm about to teach you). Let's begin.

WHAT IS A CANDLESTICK PATTERN AND HOW DOES IT WORK?

It's said that Japanese candlestick patterns originated from a Japanese rice trader called Munehisa Homma during the 1700s.

Almost 300 years later, this concept was introduced to the Western world by

Steve Nison, in his book, *Japanese Candlestick Charting Techniques.* Now, it's likely the original ideas have been modified somewhat, leading to the candlestick patterns you see today.

Anyway, that's the brief history behind Japanese candlestick patterns. So now the question is, how do you read a Japanese candlestick chart?

Let's begin by understanding that every candlestick pattern has four data points:

Open: the opening price.

High: the highest price over a specific time period.

Low: the lowest price over a specific time period.

Close: the closing price.

Here's an example:

Figure 4.1 – Bullish and bearish candles explained

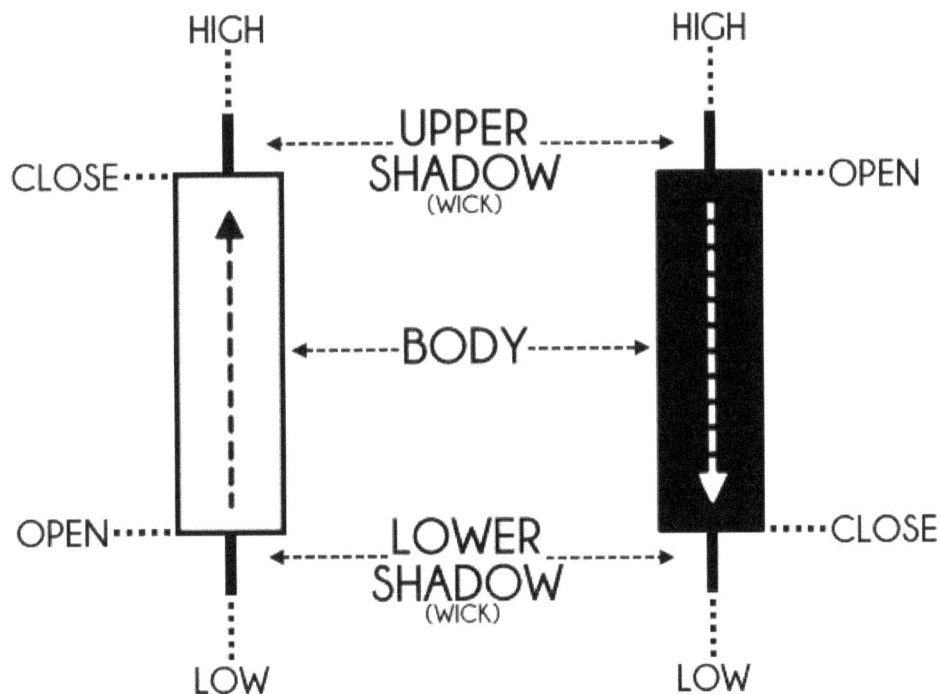

Note: For a bullish candle, the open is always below the close. And for a bearish candle, the open is always above the close.

Now that you understand the basics of candlestick patterns, let's move on and learn about reversal candlestick patterns.

BULLISH REVERSAL CANDLESTICK PATTERNS

Bullish reversal candlestick patterns signify that buyers are momentarily in control. However, this doesn't mean that you should buy immediately when you spot such a pattern because you must take the market conditions into consideration (more on that later).

For now, these are five bullish reversal candlestick patterns we'll be discussing:

- Hammer.

- Bullish engulfing pattern.

- Piercing pattern.

- Tweezer bottom.

- Morning star.

Now, there are many more bullish reversal candlestick patterns out there. But you don't need to know them all since the key focus here is just to get the gist of how to read candlestick patterns (and not to memorize any of the specific patterns). So let's get started.

Hammer

Figure 4.2 – Hammer

A hammer is a (one-candle) bullish reversal pattern that forms after a decline in price.

Here's how to recognize it:

- Little or no upper shadow.

- The price closes at the top ¼ of the range.

- The lower shadow is about two or three times the length of the body.

And this is what a hammer means:

4. When the market opened, the sellers took control and pushed the price lower.

5. At the selling climax, huge buying pressure stepped in which pushed the price higher.

6. The buying pressure was so strong that it closed above the opening price.
   In short, a hammer is a bullish reversal candlestick pattern that shows rejection of lower prices. Next…

Bullish Engulfing Pattern

A bullish engulfing pattern is a (two-candle) bullish reversal pattern that forms after a decline in price.

Here's how to recognize it:

- The first candle has a bearish close.

- The body of the second candle completely "covers" the body of the first candle (without taking into consideration the shadow).

- The second candle closes bullish.

Figure 4.3 – Bullish Engulfing Pattern

And this is what a bullish engulfing pattern means:

1. On the first candle, the sellers are in control because they closed lower for the period.

2. On the second candle, strong buying pressure stepped in and the close was above the previous candle's high, which tells you that buyers have won the battle for now.

In essence, a bullish engulfing pattern tells you that the buyers have overwhelmed the sellers and they're now in control. Next…

Piercing Pattern

A piercing pattern is a (two-candle) reversal pattern that forms after a decline in price.

Unlike the bullish engulfing pattern which closes above the previous open, the piercing pattern closes within the body of the previous candle. Thus, in terms of strength, the piercing pattern isn't as strong as the bullish engulfing pattern.

Here's how to recognize it:

- The first candle has a bearish close.
- The body of the second candle closes beyond the halfway mark of the first candle.
- The second candle closes bullish.

Figure 4.4 – Piercing Pattern

And this is what a piercing pattern means:

1. On the first candle, the sellers are in control because they closed lower for the period.
2. On the second candle, buying pressure has stepped in. and the close was bullish (more than 50% of the previous body), which tells you

there is buying pressure present. Next…

Tweezer Bottom

When I say tweezer, I don't mean the tool you use to pick your nose hairs (although it sure looks like one). Instead, a tweezer bottom is a (two-candle) reversal pattern that occurs after a decline in price.

Here's how to recognize it:

- The first candle shows rejection of lower prices.
- The second candle re-tests the low of the previous candle and closes higher.

Figure 4.5 – Tweezer Bottom

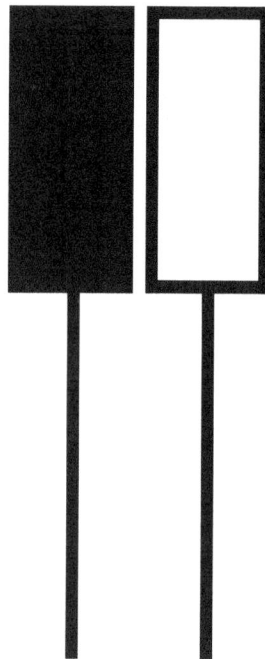

This is what a tweezer bottom means:

1. On the first candle, the sellers pushed the price lower and were met with some buying pressure.

2. On the second candle, the sellers again tried to push the price lower but failed and were finally overwhelmed by strong buying pressure.

In short, a tweezer bottom tells you the market has difficulty trading lower (after two attempts) and the price is likely to head higher. Next...

Morning Star

A morning star is a (three-candle) bullish reversal pattern that forms after a decline in price.

Here's how to recognize it:

- The first candle has a bearish close.

- The second candle has a small range.

- The third candle closes aggressively higher (at more than 50% of the first candle).

Figure 4.6 – Morning Star

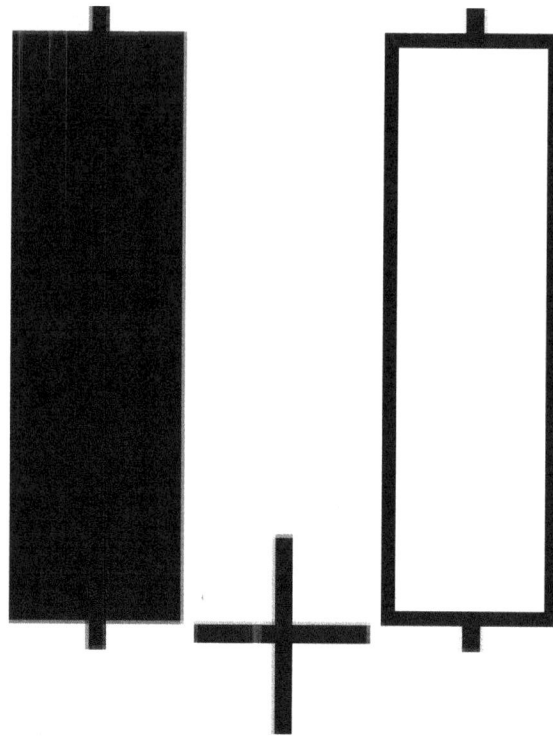

And this is what a morning star means:

1. On the first candle, the sellers are in control since the price closes lower.

2. On the second candle, there is indecision in the markets because both selling and buying pressure are in equilibrium (that's why the range of the candle is small).

3. On the third candle, the buyers have won the battle and the price closes higher.

In short, a morning star tells you that the sellers are exhausted and the buyers are momentarily in control.

Moving on, you'll learn about bearish reversal candlestick patterns, which are the opposite of what we've just covered. If you're already familiar with the materials, feel free to skip this section.

BEARISH REVERSAL CANDLESTICK PATTERNS

Bearish reversal candlestick patterns signify that sellers are momentarily in control. However, this doesn't mean you should sell immediately when you spot such a pattern because you must take the market conditions into consideration (more on that later).

For now, these are the five bearish reversal candlestick patterns that we'll be discussing:

- Shooting star
- Bearish engulfing pattern
- Dark cloud cover
- Tweezer top
- Evening star

Let's get started…

Shooting Star

A shooting star is a (one-candle) bearish reversal pattern that forms after an advance in price.

Here's how to recognize it:

- There is little or no lower shadow.
- The price closes at the bottom quarter of the range.
- The upper shadow is about two or three times the length of the body.

Figure 4.7 – Shooting Star

And this is what a shooting star means:

7. When the market opened, the buyers took control and pushed the price higher.

8. At the buying climax, huge selling pressure stepped in and pushed the price lower.

9. The selling pressure was so strong that it closed below the opening price.

   In short, a shooting star is a bearish reversal candlestick pattern that shows rejection of higher prices. Next…

Bearish Engulfing Pattern

A bearish engulfing pattern is a (two-candle) bearish reversal pattern that forms after an advance in price.

Here's how to recognize it:

- The first candle has a bullish close.

- The body of the second candle completely "covers" the body first candle (without taking into consideration the shadow).

- The second candle closes bearish.

Figure 4.8 – Bearish Engulfing Pattern

And this is what a bearish engulfing pattern means:

1. On the first candle, the buyers were in control since they closed higher for the period.

2. On the second candle, strong selling pressure stepped in and the price closed below the previous candle's low, which tells you that the sellers have won the battle for now.

In essence, a bearish engulfing pattern tells you the sellers have overwhelmed the buyers and are now in control. Next…

Dark Cloud Cover

A dark cloud cover is a (two-candle) reversal pattern that forms after an advance in price. Unlike the bearish engulfing pattern that closes below the previous open, the dark cloud cover closes within the body of the previous candle. Thus, in terms of strength, dark cloud cover isn't as strong as the bearish engulfing pattern.

Here's how to recognize it:

- The first candle has a bullish close.
- The body of the second candle closes beyond the halfway mark of the first candle.
- The second candle closes bearish.

Figure 4.9 – Dark Cloud Cover

And this is what a dark cloud cover means:

1. On the first candle, the buyers are in control because they closed higher

for the period.

2. On the second candle, selling pressure stepped in and the price closed bearishly (more than 50% of the previous body), which tells you there is some selling pressure.

Next...

Tweezer Top

A tweezer top is a (two-candle) reversal pattern that occurs after an advance in price.

Here's how to recognize it:

- The first candle shows rejection of higher prices.
- The second candle re-tests the high of the previous candle and closes lower.

Figure 4.10 – Tweezer Top

And this is what a tweezer top means:

1. On the first candle, the buyers pushed the price higher and were met with some selling pressure.

2. On the second candle, the buyers again tried to push the price higher but failed and were finally overwhelmed by strong selling pressure.

In short, a tweezer top tells you the market has difficulty trading higher (after two attempts) and it's likely to head lower. Next…

Evening Star

An evening star is a (three-candle) bearish reversal pattern that forms after an advance in price.

Here's how to recognize it:

- The first candle has a bullish close.

- The second candle has a small range.
- The third candle closes aggressively lower (more than 50% of the first candle).

Figure 4.11 – Evening Star

And this is what an evening star means:

1. The first candle shows the buyers are in control as the price closes higher.

2. On the second candle, there is indecision in the markets because both the selling and buying pressure are in equilibrium (that's why the range of the candle is small).

3. On the third candle, the sellers won the battle and the price closed lower.

In short, an evening star tells you the buyers are exhausted, and the sellers are momentarily in control.

Now, the purpose of going through these individual patterns is to teach you how to analyze them step by step. You might be thinking, "Gosh, there are so many candlestick patterns to learn!"

Don't worry because you're about to learn a simple technique that will help you understand any candlestick pattern that comes your way—even if you don't know the name of it. Here's how.

HOW TO UNDERSTAND ANY CANDLESTICK PATTERNS WITHOUT MEMORIZING A SINGLE ONE

All you need to do is ask yourself these two questions:

1. Where did the price close relative to the range?

Look at this candlestick pattern:

Figure 4.12 – Weak price rejection

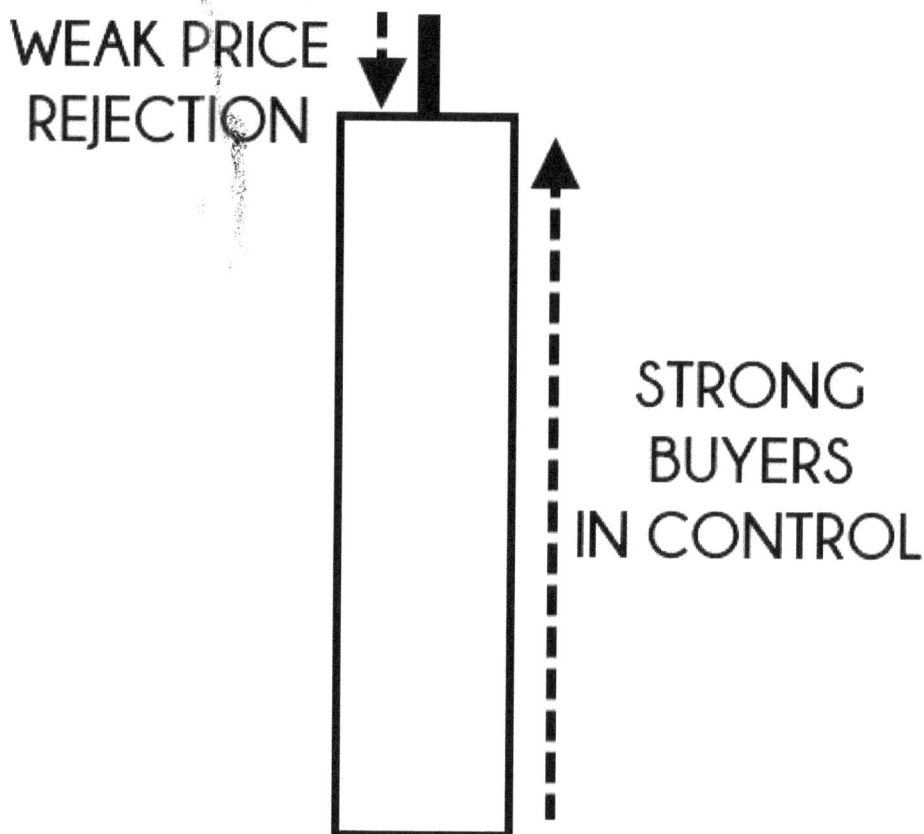

Who's in control? Well, the price closed the near highs of the range, which tells you the buyers are in control. Next, look at this candlestick pattern:

Figure 4.13 – Strong price rejection

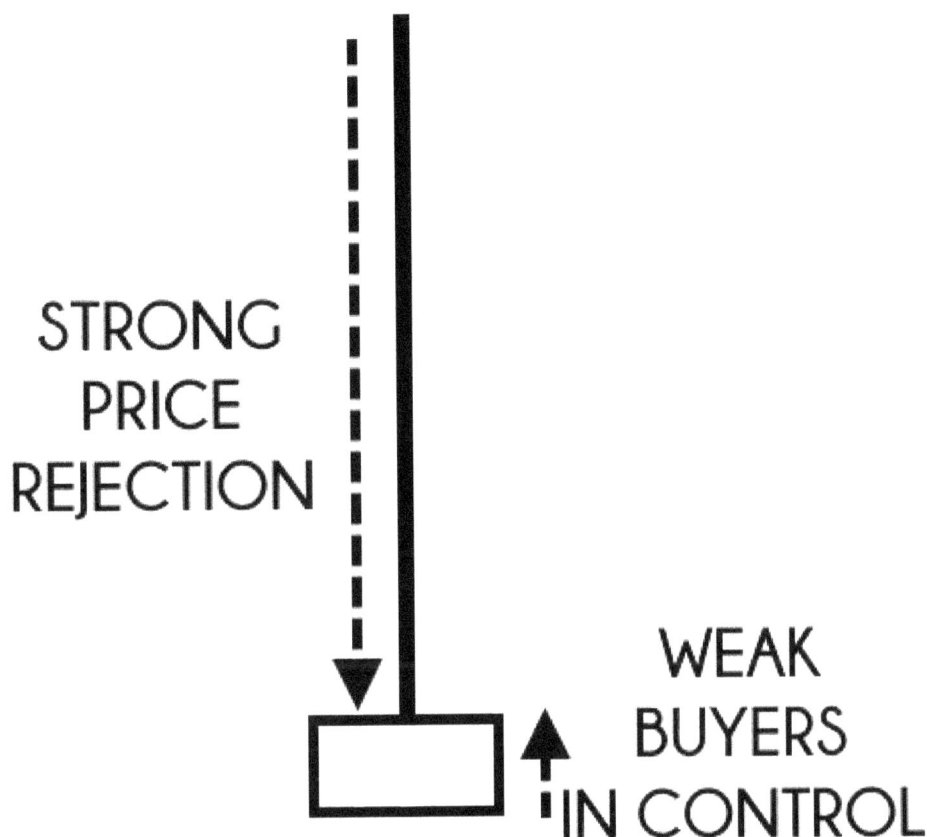

Who's in control? Although it's a bullish candle, the sellers are actually the ones in control. Why? Because the price closed near the lows of the range and shows rejection of higher prices.

So remember, if you want to know who's in control, ask yourself, "Where did the price close relative to the range?"

Moving on…

2. What's the size of the candlestick pattern relative to the earlier ones?

This question will help you determine if there's any strength (or conviction) behind the move. So what you want to do is compare the size of the current candle to the earlier ones. If the current candle is much larger (like two or more times larger), this tells you there's strength behind the move.

Here's an example:

Figure 4.14 – Large Bullish Engulfing Pattern (GBP/CAD Daily)

If there's no strength behind the move, the size of the current candle is about the same as the earlier ones. This is what I mean:

Figure 4.15 – Small Bullish Engulfing Pattern (EUR/CAD 4-hour)

Does this make sense to you? Great! You can now read and understand any candlestick patterns like a pro. It doesn't matter if it's a doji, a spinning top, a harami, three white soldiers, or any other kind of pattern. You have what it takes.

AT THIS POINT…

You've learned a ton about candlestick patterns, what they are, how they work, and how to understand any candlestick pattern without having to memorize any of them. But wait, what's the purpose of candlestick patterns?

Well, candlestick patterns are useful as entry triggers to help you time your entry. Recall that market structure tells you what to do. Support and resistance (or the area of value) tells you where to trade. And candlestick patterns tell you *when* to enter.

I hope you're starting to see the picture I'm trying to paint. But before we dive into trading strategies, there's one more critical component I must cover, so read on.

SUMMARY

- Candlestick patterns give you an idea of who's currently in control of the markets.

- There are three types of candlestick patterns: reversal, indecision, and continuation.

- If you want to know who's currently in control of the markets, ask yourself, "Where did the price close relative to the range?"

- If you want to know if there's strength behind a move, ask yourself, "What's the size of the candlestick pattern relative to the earlier ones?"

- Candlestick patterns are useful as entry triggers to time your entries.

- Don't trade candlestick patterns in isolation. You must take into account the context of the markets (and aspects like market structure and area of value).

THE SECRET TO RISK AND TRADE MANAGEMENT

During the 2008 financial crisis, I knew of a trader who made a million dollars a year trading on the futures market. He traded large, putting on a few hundred contracts at a time, and it was not uncommon to see his P&L swing six figures up and down—within a day.

Can you guess what he is doing right now? He drives a cab for a living. Now, don't get me wrong, I've got nothing against cab drivers. The point I'm trying to make is this: You can trade like a king and make sick money, but if you don't manage your risk, it's only a matter of time before you lose it all.

Paul Tudor Jones once said, "The most important rule of trading is to play great defense, not great offence." This couldn't be truer, and that's why I've dedicated an entire chapter to helping you manage your risk so you can survive in this business.

So in this section, you'll learn the truth about stop hunting, how to set a proper stop loss, apply proper risk management to your trading, calculate the optimal position size for your trades, and how to manage your trades to capture a swing or ride massive trends. Sound good? Then let's roll…

HOW THE SMART MONEY HUNTS YOUR STOP LOSS

The market exists to facilitate transactions between buyers and sellers. The more buyers and sellers transact, the more efficient the market will be. This leads to greater liquidity (the ease of which buying/selling can occur without moving the markets).

If you're a retail trader, liquidity is hardly an issue for you since your size is small. But for an institution, liquidity is the main concern. Imagine this:

You manage a hedge fund, and you want to buy one million shares of ABC stock. You know support is at $100 and ABC stock is trading at $110. If you were to enter the market, you'd likely push the price higher and get filled at an average price of $115. That's $5 higher than the current price. So what do you do?

Well, you know $100 is an area of support, and chances are there'll be a cluster of stop-loss positions below this (from traders who are long on ABC stock).

So if you can push the price lower to trigger these stops, there'll be a flood of sell orders hitting the market (since traders who are long will exit their losing position).

With the amount of selling pressure coming in, you could buy your one million shares of ABC stock from these traders. This gives you a better entry price than hitting the market and suffering a $5 slippage.

In other words, if an institution wants to long the markets with minimal slippage, they tend to place a sell order to trigger nearby stop losses.

This allows them to buy from traders, thereby cutting their losses, which offers them a more favorable entry price. Look at your charts, and you'll often see the market taking out the lows of support, only to trade higher subsequently.

Here's an example:

Figure 5.1 – The price traded below support before reversing higher (EUR/JPY 4-hour)

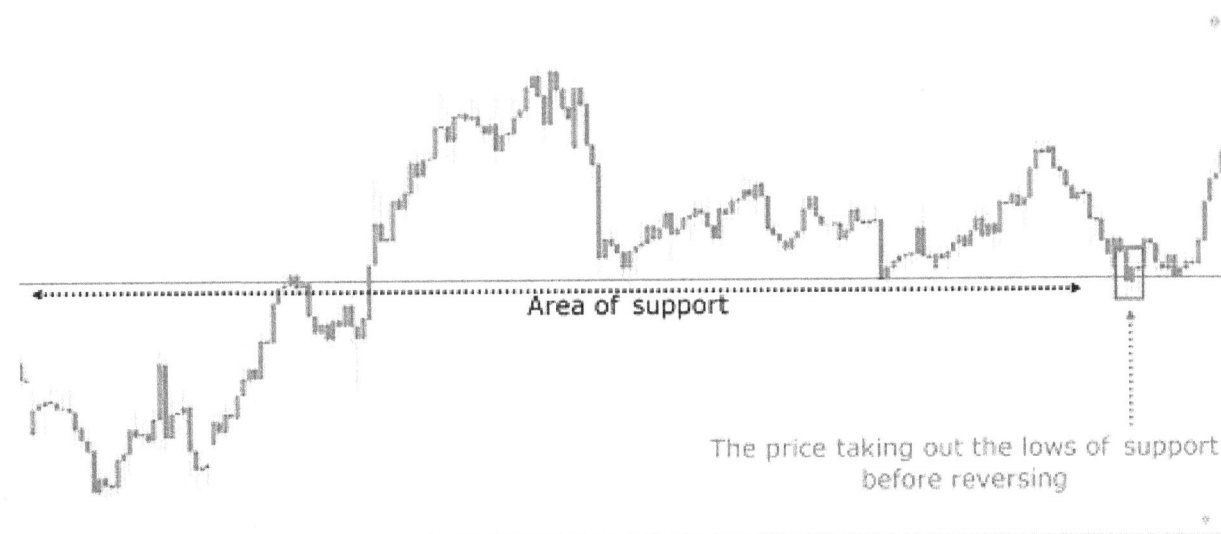

Area of support

The price taking out the lows of support before reversing

This means you don't want to set your stop loss just below the lows of support or above the highs of resistance because it's easy to get stop hunted. Also, you don't want to set your stop loss based on how you feel or how much money is left in your account because the market doesn't care about any of these things. So what now?

HOW TO SET A PROPER STOP LOSS

When you set your stop loss, you want to have a "barrier" working in your favor to prevent the price from moving against you. These "barriers" can be things like support and resistance, swing highs and lows, trendlines, etc.

This means that when you set a stop loss, you want to lean against an area of value because the market will face difficulty breaking through. Make sense? Great. Here's how to do it.

First, identify the area of value. Then add a "buffer" to it so you don't get stopped out just because the price spiked through the lows of support.

For an example, let's say your area of value is at support, so what you'll do is identify the lows of support and subtract 1 ATR from the lows (for short trades, you add 1 ATR to the highs of resistance).

Here's what I mean:

Figure 5.2 – Set your stop loss 1 ATR below support (EUR/GBP Daily)

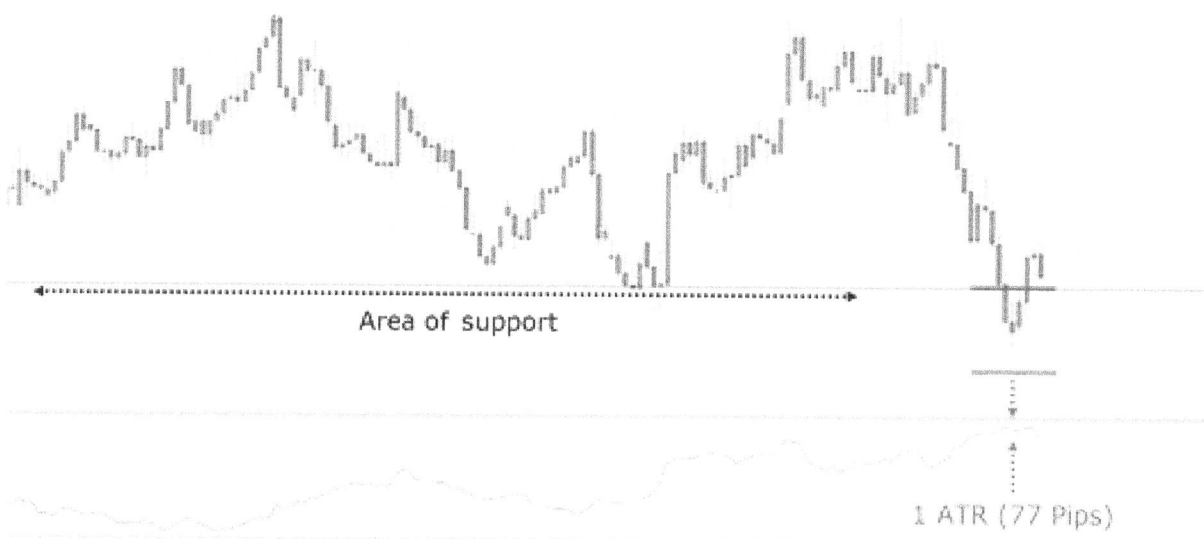

Area of support

1 ATR (77 Pips)

Also, when you set a stop loss, it should be at a level that invalidates your trading setup. For example, if you're buying the breakout of a bull flag, your stop loss should be below the lows of the bull flag because anywhere above it, the bull flag pattern is still intact. But below its lows, the bull flag is "destroyed," and your trading setup is invalidated. Next, you'll learn how to calculate the optimal position size of your trades so you don't blow up your account. Let's go…

RISK MANAGEMENT: HOW TO CALCULATE POSITION SIZE (FOREX)

The secret to risk management lies in this diagram below:

Figure 5.3 – Risk of ruin table

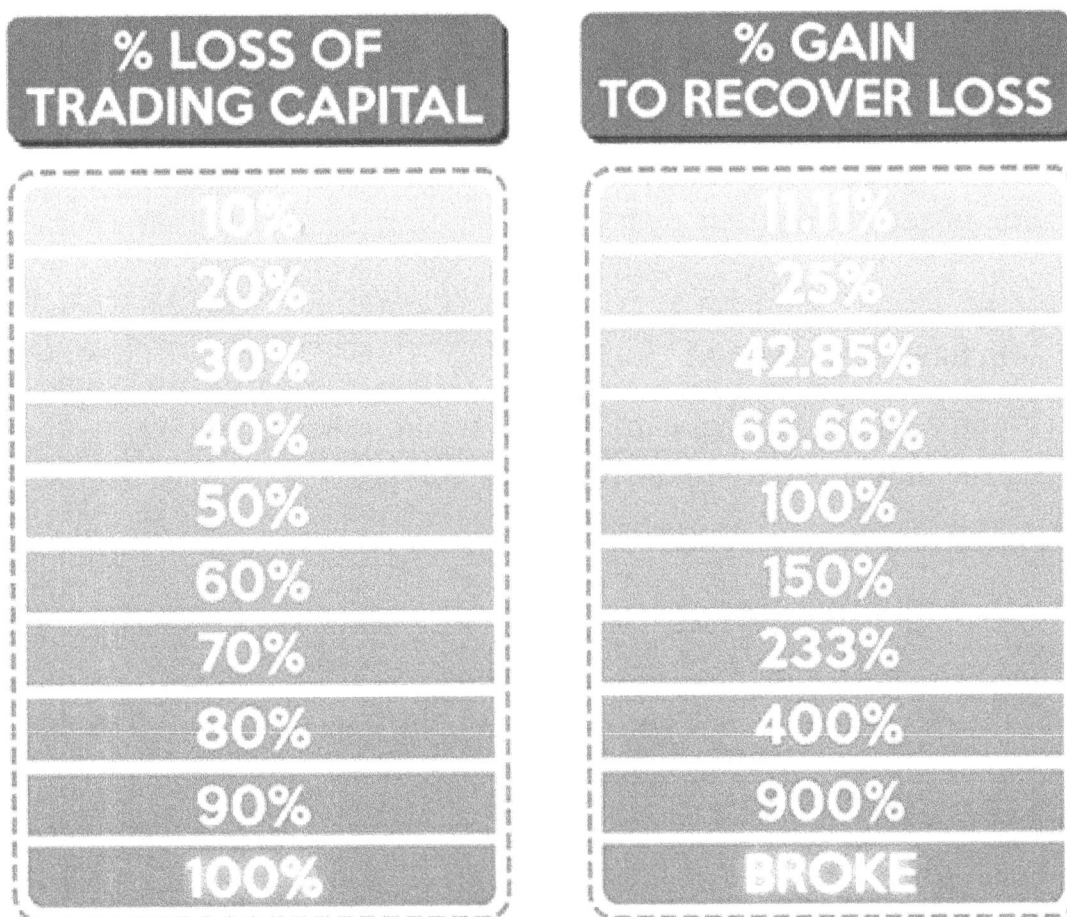

% LOSS OF TRADING CAPITAL	% GAIN TO RECOVER LOSS
10%	11.11%
20%	25%
30%	42.85%
40%	66.66%
50%	100%
60%	150%
70%	233%
80%	400%
90%	900%
100%	BROKE

As you can see, if you lose 10% of your trading capital, you'll need to earn 11.11% to get back to breakeven. If you lose 50% of your capital, you'll need a 100% return to get back to breakeven. And if you hit a drawdown of 90%, you'll need a return of 900% before you break even (good luck with that).

The secret to risk management is to lose small when you're wrong so you never hit a level of drawdown that's impossible to recover from. That's why you want to risk a fraction of your capital on every trade (my suggestion is not more than 1%). This means if you have 20 losing trades in a row, your drawdown will be about 20%. This won't be the end of the world, and you can still live to fight another day.

Now the question is, how many units do you trade if you only want to risk 1% of your trading account? Here's the formula for forex trading:

*Position size = Amount you're risking / (stop loss * value per pip)*

Let me give you an example:

10. You have a trading account that's worth $10,000 USD and you risk 1% on each trade (which is $100).

11. You want to short GBP/USD at 1.2700 because it's a resistance area.

12. You have a stop loss of 200 pips.

13. Value per pip for 1 standard lot = $10 USD/pip.
    Plug the numbers into the formula and you get:

    Position size = 100 / (200*10)

    = 0.05 lot (or five micro lots)

    This means you can trade five micro-lots on GBP/USD with a stop loss of 200 pips. And if it hits your stop loss, the loss on this trade is $100 (which is 1% of your trading account), excluding slippage. Now, what about stocks?

HOW TO CALCULATE POSITION SIZE (FOR STOCKS)

The formula for stocks is slightly different, but the concept is the same:

Position size = amount you're risking/(size of your stop loss)

Let me give you an example:

1. You have a $50,000 USD trading account, and you're risking 1% on each trade (which is $500).

2. You want to go long on McDonald's at 118.5 because it's an area of support.

3. You have a stop loss of $2.50.

So how many shares of McDonald's can you buy?

Plug the numbers into the formula and you get:

Position size = 500 / 2.5

= 200 shares

This means you can buy 200 shares of McDonald's with a stop loss of $2.50. If it's triggered, the loss on this trade is $500 (which is 1% of your trading account).

You don't have to calculate your position size manually because there are position size calculators to help you do this. If you're interested, you can get one here: priceactiontradingsecrets.com/bonus

So you've learned how to manage your risk and take care of your downside. But if the market moves in your favor, what's next? How do you know when to exit your winners? That's what you're going to learn next.

TRADE EXITS: HOW TO CAPTURE A SWING

A swing refers to "one move" in the markets. The idea of capturing a swing (also known as swing trading) is to exit your winners before opposing pressure comes in. Here's an example:

Figure 5.4 – Capturing a swing

The advantage of capturing a swing is that you endure "less pain" because you exit your trade before the market reverses against you. This improves your consistency and your winning rate. But the downside is that you'll miss big moves in the market as you exit your trades too early.

So if this approach is for you, then the key thing is to exit your trades before opposing pressure steps in. This means if you're long, you'll want to exit your trade before selling pressure comes in. And where would that be? Possibly at swing lows, support, the lower channel, etc.

Here's an example:

Figure 5.5 – Exiting your trade before channel support as buying pressure could push the price higher

Channel resistance

Channel support

TRADE EXITS: HOW TO RIDE A TREND

The only way you'll ever ride a trend is to use a trailing stop loss. This means you progressively shift your stop loss higher as the market moves in your favor. Here's what I mean:

Figure 5.6 – Riding a trend

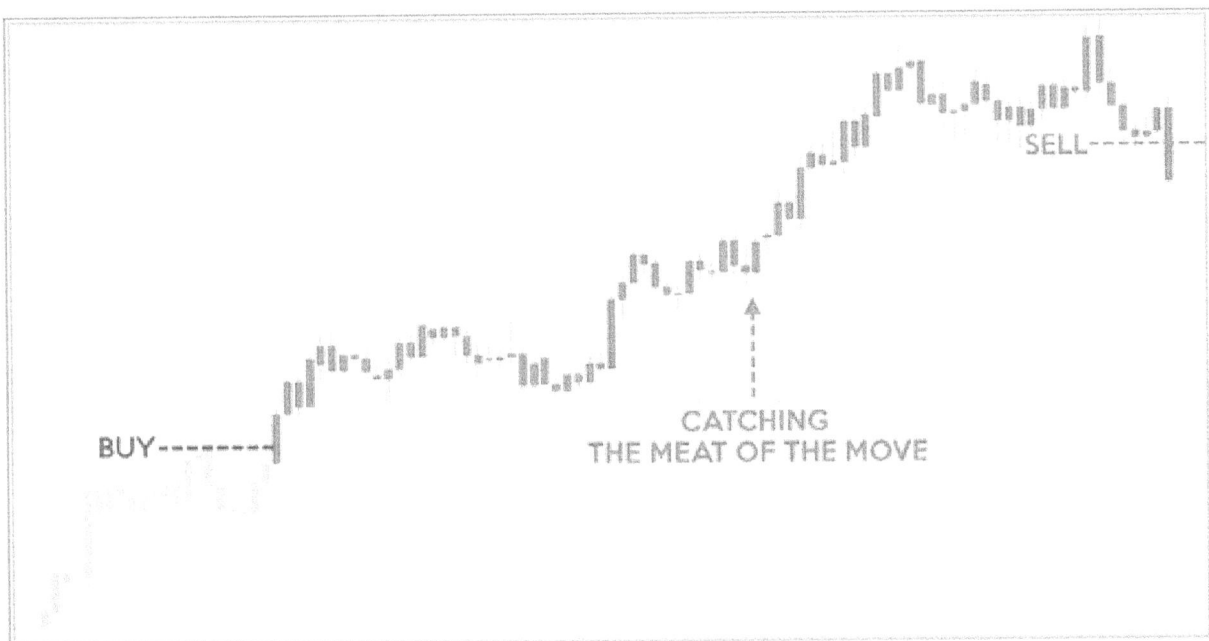

BUY--------

CATCHING
THE MEAT OF THE MOVE

SELL-----

The beauty of riding a trend is that you can reap massive profits doing little to no work. You can expect your average gains to be two-to-three times larger than your losses. But, there's always a but, right? The downside is that you'll only win 30%-45% of the time, you could give back 30%-50% of your open profits, and it's common to have your winners turn to losers.

Psychologically, riding a trend is one of the most difficult things for traders to do. But if this approach is for you, the key is to embrace your losses and adopt a proper trailing stop-loss technique. So how do you trail your stop loss? There are many ways to do this, like moving average, average true range, market structure, etc.

Moving Average

Let me give you an example using moving average. If you want to ride a long-term uptrend, you can trail your stop loss with the 200-day moving average. This means you'll only exit the trade if the price closes below the 200-day moving average; otherwise, you hold onto it (and it's just the opposite for a downtrend). Here's an example:

Figure 5.7 – Trailing your stop loss using the 200-day moving average (USD/TRY Daily)

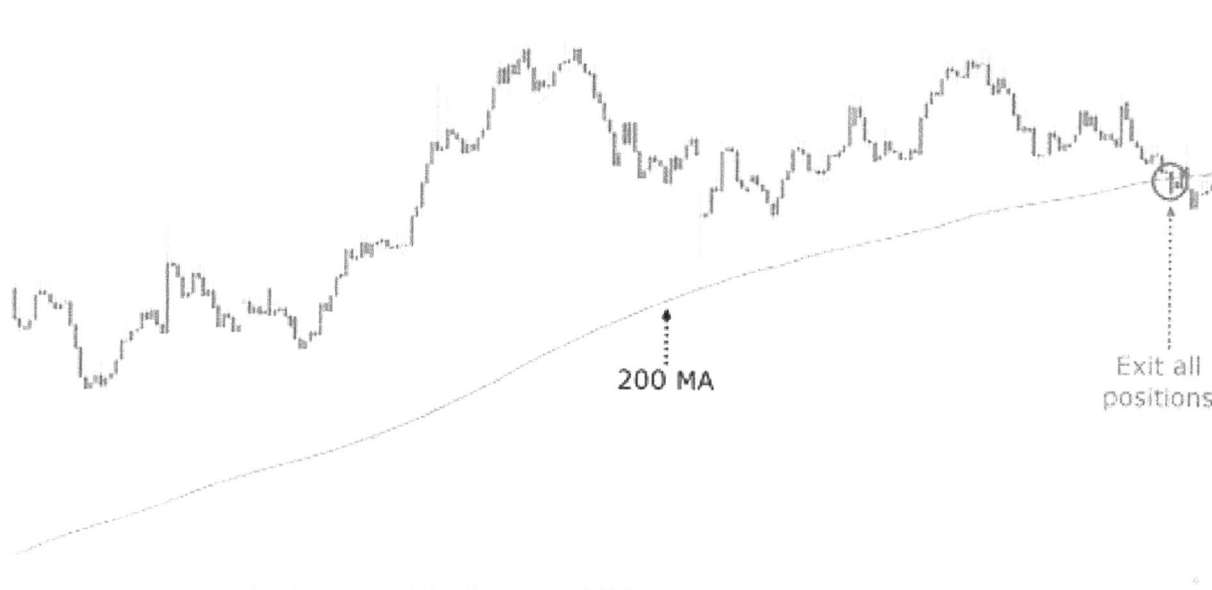

200 MA

Exit all positions

In addition, you can tweak the moving average to accommodate the type of trend you want to capture. If you want to ride a medium-term trend, you can trail your stop loss with the 100-day moving average. Or, if you want to ride a longer term trend, you can use the 300-day moving average.

Market Structure

Another way to trail your stop loss is by using market structure. As you know, an uptrend consists of higher highs and lows. So what you do is trail your stop loss using the previous swing low. This means if the price closes below the previous swing low (by more than one 1 ATR), you'll exit the trade (and vice versa for a downtrend). Here's what I mean:

Figure 5.8 – Trailing your stop loss using market structure (EUR/USD Daily)

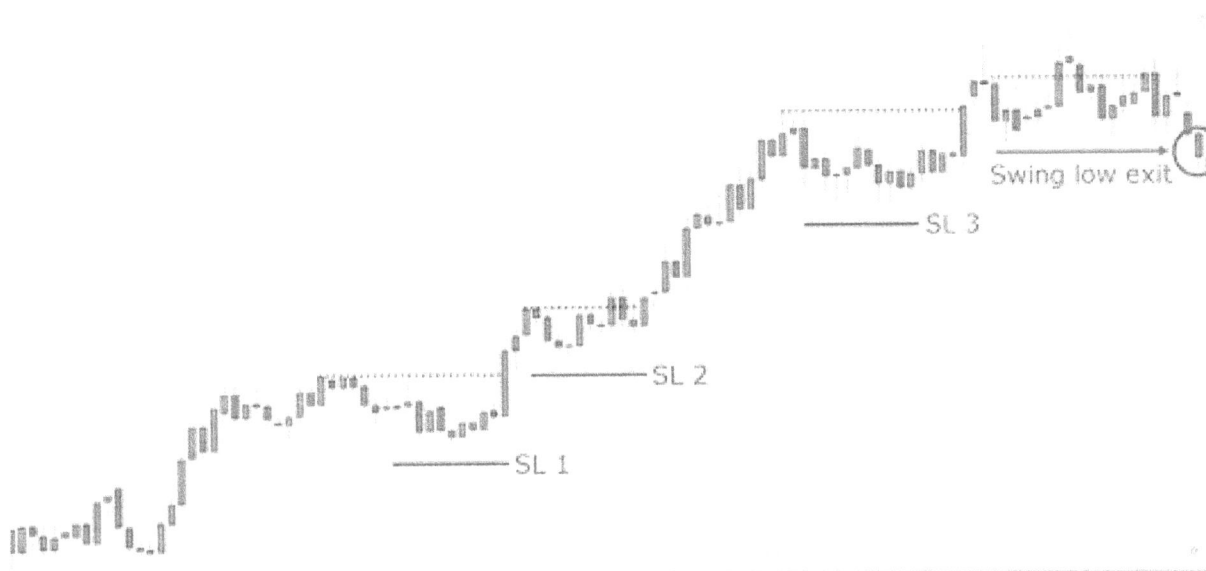

Unlike moving average, market structure is subjective because it requires discretion when you're identifying the swing highs/lows. So if you prefer something more objective, use moving average to trail your stop loss.

TRADE EXITS: HYBRID APPROACH

Finally, you can combine both approaches to capture a swing and ride a trend. Here's how it works. Let's say you're in a long position and the market has come into an area of resistance. You're not sure if the price could break out higher or not. So what now? Do you take all your profits and just capture a swing? And what if the price breaks out higher and you miss a good chunk of the move?

Well, what you can do is sell some of your position at resistance and hold the remaining portion to see if the price breaks out higher. If it does, you'll have the potential to ride the trend higher. If the price doesn't break out higher but reverses instead, then you'll get stopped out on the remaining position. But at least your earlier position closed at a profit (and this will subsidize some of your losses).

Now, if you want to adopt this approach, my suggestion is to exit no more than 50% of your position for the first target because if you exit with anything more than that, the remaining position won't make much of a difference to your bottom line.

For example, if you exit 90% of your position at resistance and hold onto the remaining 10%, even if your remaining position gives you a 1:10 risk-to-reward ratio, the net profit is only a gain of 1R (since it's 10% of your original position size).

What about the downsides? Well, there are two: **1.** If the market trends well, you'll never have your full position size on because a portion of it was exited earlier. **2.** If the price hits your first target and reverses, you might end up at breakeven or experience a small loss. But had you chosen a swing trading approach, that trade would have been a winner.

By now you should realize that there's no best method, strategy, technique, or whatever in trading. There are always pros and cons with any action you choose. So the key isn't finding the holy grail but finding a method you can embrace and execute consistently.

AT THIS POINT...

You've learned the essentials of risk and trade management. Specifically, we've covered how to avoid stop hunting, how to set a proper stop loss, how to calculate your optimal position size, and how to exit your trade to capture a swing or ride a trend. Whew!

Now, this is where things get interesting because we're going to put the pieces of the puzzle together so everything makes sense to you (I promise). So read on.

SUMMARY

- You can have the best trading strategy in the world, but without proper risk management, you will eventually blow up your trading account.

- Your stop loss should lean against an area of value which acts as a "barrier" to prevent the price from moving against you.

- The wider your stop loss, the smaller your position size will be (if you want to risk the same percentage of your account on each trade).

- If you want to capture a swing, then look to exit your trade before the opposing pressure steps in.

- If you want to ride a trend, you need to trail your stop loss as the price moves in your favor.

TRADING FORMULAS: HOW TO DEVELOP WINNING STRATEGIES TO BEAT THE MARKETS

Stop! If you've jumped ahead to this chapter because you saw the word "strategies," then please stop reading because this chapter builds on the foundations that were covered earlier in the book. So if you haven't read the earlier sections, stop right now and go back to page one. But if you've followed everything, then this is where the "magic" happens.

After I completed my national service, I wanted to further my studies. So I enrolled at the University of London (UOL), where I studied banking and finance. Now, I didn't want to "smoke my way" through university by doing the least possible amount of work. Nope. I wanted to graduate with First Class Honours and make my parents proud (if you're unaware of my history, I had been an academically weak student throughout my teenage years). I had to make it happen. So what did I do?

I went all in! I studied everything I could get my hands on: Google, YouTube, library books, past year exam papers – everything. And one thing I realized was that I couldn't just "blindly" memorize questions and answers because there were so many variations on what I was learning. And UOL is known for giving poor marks if your answers look like they were created from a template. So what did I do?

I figured the only way to get First Class Honours was to truly understand the subject matter. That meant I couldn't rely on memorizing stuff; I had to understand the concepts behind what I was learning. So I focused on learning the concepts—understanding the *why* instead of the how. Did it work? Fortunately, I can say yes! Because in 2012, I graduated with First Class Honours and finished second in my cohort.

So why am I sharing this with you?

Well, it's the same with trading! You've got to focus on the concepts, not the specific strategies or tactics. The reason is simple: Once you've mastered the concepts, then nothing can trick you because you will know why something works (not just how). This means you can develop trading strategies to fit your style—and not be swayed by the "latest" trading systems that fool many traders.

So instead of spoon-feeding you specific trading strategies, I'd rather teach you trading formulas, explain the concepts behind them, and show you how you can use these formulas to develop your own trading strategies. And that's what you're about to discover right now. Let's begin.

THE MAEE FORMULA

First, let me introduce you to the MAEE formula (which is about trading price reversals). MAEE stands for market structure, area of value, entry trigger, and exits. And if you haven't realized it yet, these are the individual components we covered earlier (if you haven't read about these, please stop and go back to page one). Here's how it works:

Market Structure: the first thing you want to do is identify the current market structure, so you'll know *what* to do. Ask yourself, "Is this in an accumulation, advancing, distribution, or declining stage?" Now, there are times when it's impossible to classify the market structure, and if that's the case, move on to something else; don't force your analysis on the charts.

Area of Value: next, you want to identify the area of value so you know *where* to enter a trade. This can be things like support and resistance, trendlines, channels, etc. For example, if you're looking for buying opportunities, you'll want to ask yourself, "Where might potential buying pressure step in?"

Entry Trigger: then, you'll want to have an entry trigger so you'll know *when* to enter a trade. We covered an entire section on candlestick patterns because they're useful for identifying entry triggers. So if you're looking for buying opportunities, you can look for candlestick patterns like the hammer, the bullish engulfing pattern, and so on. Now, don't limit yourself only to candlestick patterns because there are other types of entry triggers. These can be chart patterns, indicators crossing a certain value, etc. (The point is, keep an open mind and always keep learning.)

Exits: finally, you have exits so you know *when* to exit a trade. There are two parts to this: 1) Exit when the price moves against you (otherwise known as a stop loss); 2) Exit when the price moves in your favor (you can do this using target profit or trailing stop loss).

Now let me walk you through a few examples:

Figure 6.1 – MAEE Formula Example 1 (GBP/USD Daily)

GBPUSD is in a declining stage (market structure) with a series of lower highs and lows. The price did a pullback towards resistance at 1.2750 (area of value) and formed a bearish engulfing pattern (entry trigger). You could set your stop loss 1 ATR above the highs of resistance (exit when you're wrong) and have a target profit at the nearest swing low, which is around 1.2550 area (exit when you're right).

Figure 6.2 – MAEE Formula Example 2 (Copper 8-hour)

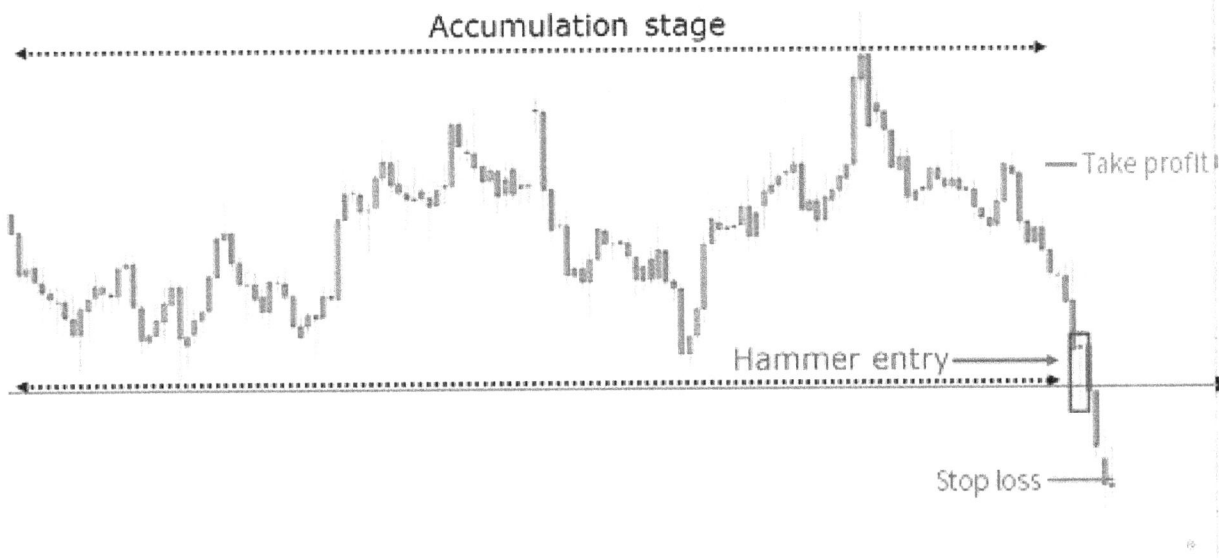

Copper is in a potential accumulation stage (market structure). The price collapsed to support at 2.600 (area of value) and formed a hammer (entry trigger). You could have your stop loss 1 ATR below the lows of the hammer (exit when you're wrong) and have a target profit at the nearest swing high, which is around the 2.720 area (exit when you're right).

Figure 6.3 – MAEE Formula Example 3 (AUD/JPY Daily)

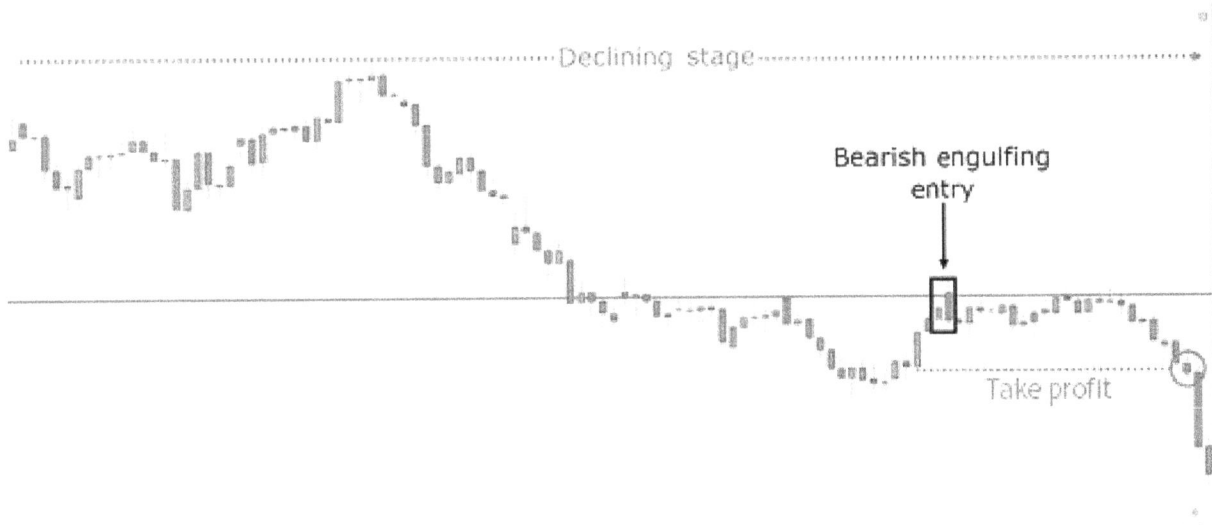

AUDJPY is in a declining stage (market structure). The price did a pullback toward the 76.00 resistance (area of value) and then gapped up higher before forming a bearish engulfing pattern (entry trigger). You could set your stop loss 1 ATR above the highs of resistance (exit when you're wrong) and have a target profit at the nearest swing low, which is around the 74.50 area (exit when you're right).

Here's the thing. The MAEE formula is not cast in stone because you can tweak it to suit your needs. For example, if you don't want to use support as an area of value, then consider something else, like moving average, trendline, etc. Likewise, you don't have to use candlestick patterns to define your entry trigger. You could go with something simple like a "higher close," or when the RSI indicator crosses above 30, etc. Again, it's up to you to figure out and validate what works for you.

Now to illustrate my point, here's another variation of the MAEE formula:

Figure 6.4a – MAEE Formula Example 4 (NZD/USD Daily)

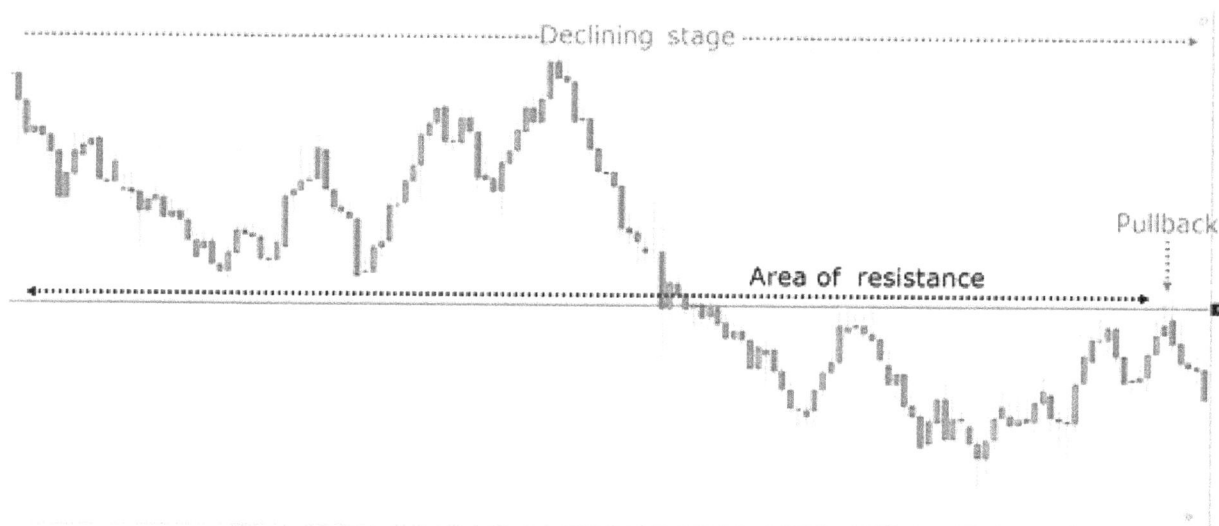

NZDUSD is in a declining stage (market structure) and the price has pullback towards resistance at 0.6450 (area of value).

Figure 6.4b – MAEE Formula Example 4 (NZD/USD 4-hour)

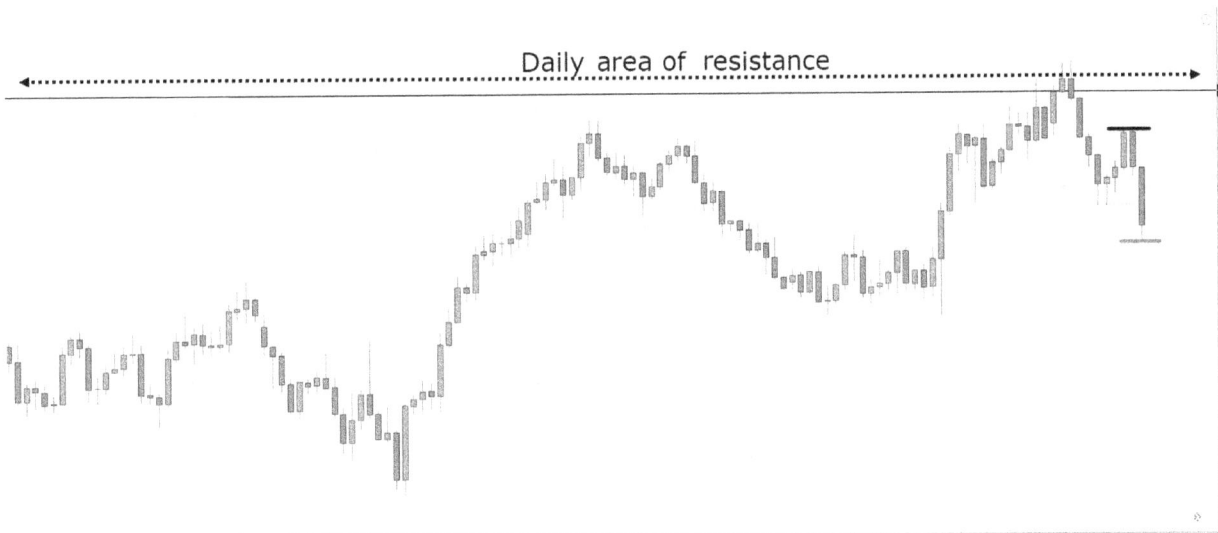

Daily area of resistance

In the 4-hour time frame, you'll notice the price formed a lower high and low, which signals the sellers are in control. So when the price breaks the swing low, that can be an entry trigger to go short. Again, your stop loss is 1 ATR above resistance (exit when you're wrong).

Figure 6.4c – MAEE Formula Example 4 (NZD/USD 4-hour)

Now, what about exiting your winners? Well, you can use a fixed target profit like we discussed earlier, or you can adopt a trailing stop loss. For example, you can trail your stop loss using the previous day's high. So if the price breaks and closes above the previous day's highs, then you'll exit the trade (exit when you're wrong). Otherwise, you can hold onto the trade and ride the move lower for as long it goes, until it hits your trailing stop loss.

BONUS TIPS (MAEE FORMULA)

Before we move on, I want to share a few important things to keep in mind when you trade using the MAEE formula. On the surface, you know what to look for. But if you dive deeper, there are a few "secret ingredients" that will dramatically improve the quality of your trading setups. These took me years to figure out, and you're about to discover them right now.

1. Power move into an area of value

This looks like big-bodied candles coming into an area of value (with little-or-no pullback). I know this sounds like a contradiction, so let me explain. When you get a strong momentum move lower, it's because there isn't enough buying pressure to hold up the price. That's why the price drops lower to find new buyers.

The "down move" is called a liquidity gap (a lack of interest) because not many transactions took place on the decline. In other words, the market can easily reverse and start moving in the opposite direction due to a lack of interest around the price level—and that's why you often see a power move down into support, and then BOOM, the price does a 180-degree reversal. Here's an example:

Figure 6.5 – Power move into support (Gold Daily)

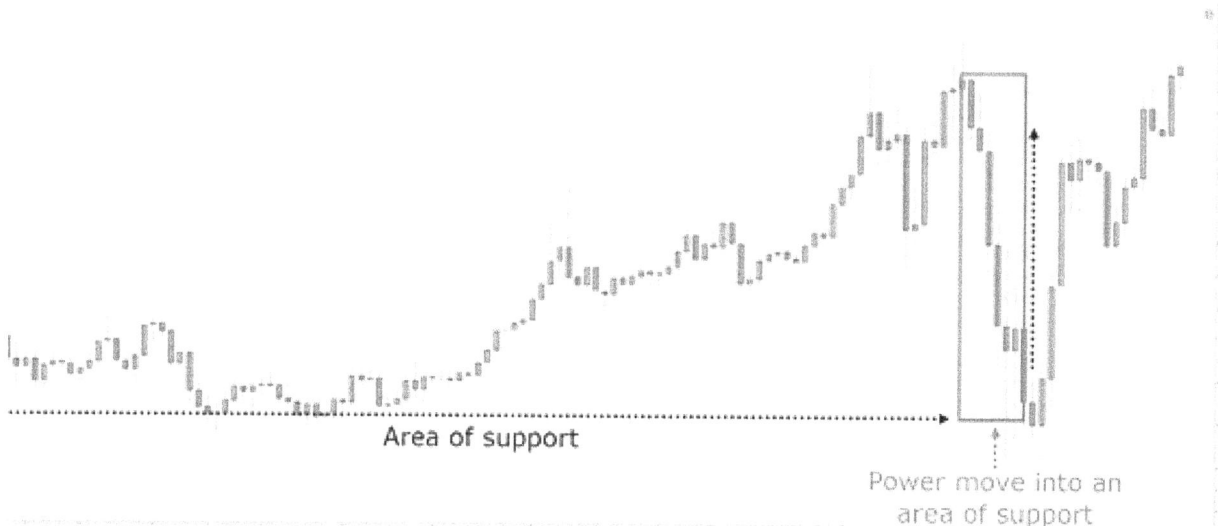

Area of support

Power move into an area of support

Also, when you trade the reversal after a power move into support, the nearest swing high is likely some distance away—and this offers you a more favorable risk-to-reward ratio.

2. Strong price rejection

For example, let's say you're looking for selling opportunities. When you identify your entry trigger, you want the range of the candle to be large (at least 1.5 times ATR), and the price closing near the lows. This signals there's strong price rejection. Here's an example:

Figure 6.6 – Strong bearish price rejection (GBP/JPY Daily)

And here's an example of a weak price rejection:

Figure 6.7 – Weak bearish price rejection (GBP/JPY Daily)

See the difference?

3. The more significant the area, the stronger the reversal

These areas (or levels) are the most obvious ones on your charts. They could be multi-year highs/lows, areas that haven't been tested in a long time, or areas that previously led to strong reversals. But why pay attention to these?

Because these areas attract attention from both breakout and reversal traders. Imagine, the price breaks out higher and breakout traders go long hoping to capture a piece of the move. As you know, not all breakouts are successful, and the ones that reverse will put breakout traders in the red. And when the price declines further, it'll hit their stop losses, which puts strong selling pressure on the markets—and this is great for trading the MAEE formula. Moving on…

THE MBEE FORMULA

The MBEE formula is about trading breakouts. MBEE stands for market structure, buildup, entry trigger, and exits. Now, you're probably familiar with all of the individual components except buildup, so let me explain what that is. A buildup looks like a series of narrow range candles (or a tight consolidation).

You're probably wondering, "But why look for a buildup?" A buildup occurs when the market's volatility is low. This means your stop loss is tighter, which offers you a more favorable risk-to-reward ratio on your trade (especially if volatility expands in your favor). So let me illustrate the MBEE formula with a few examples.

Figure 6.8 – MBEE Formula Example 1 (USD/CNH Daily)

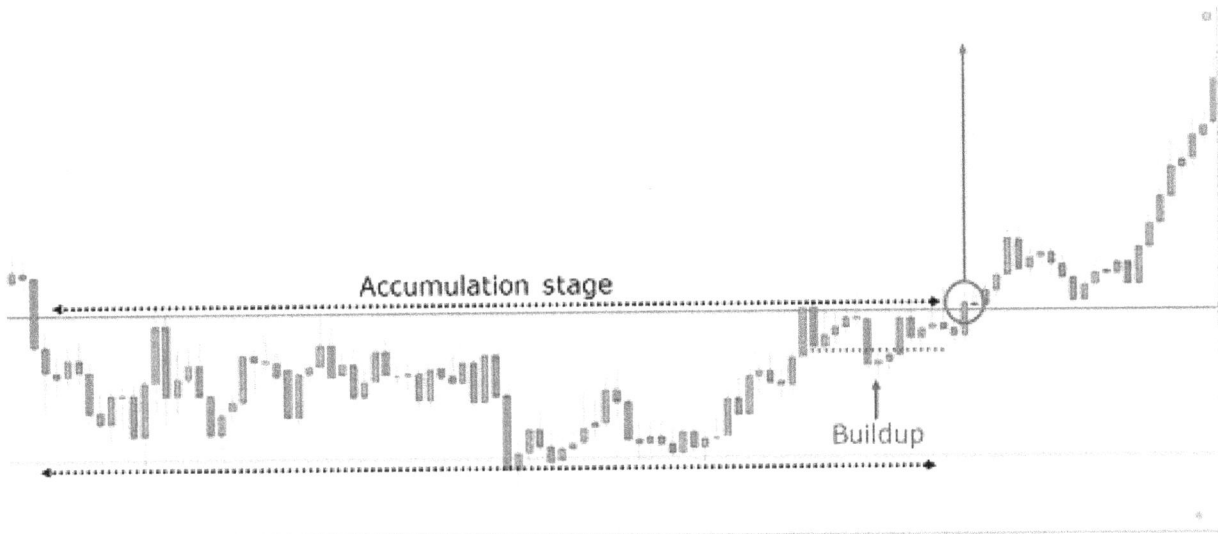

Accumulation stage

Buildup

USDCNH is in a potential accumulation stage (market structure). I use the word "potential" because you never know if the price will break out higher or continue the downtrend. Next, there's a buildup formed around the 6.3700 resistance area. This tells you one of two things: 1)The buyers are willing to buy at higher prices, even at resistance; or 2) there's a lack of selling pressure, and that's why the price is unable to move lower. Whatever the case, this is a sign of strength.

So to trade the breakout, you can go long with a buy stop order above the highs of resistance (entry trigger). Your stop loss goes 1 ATR below the lows of the buildup (exit when you're wrong) and you can trail your stop loss to ride the potential trend (exit when you're right).

Now, I prefer to use a trailing stop because this could possibly move into the advancing stage, which offers huge profit potential. Of course, you must decide what's best for you. Don't just blindly copy what I do. Also, I didn't specify which trailing stop loss technique to use because that's something you can decide for yourself. Remember, the *why* is more important than the how.

Figure 6.9 – MBEE Formula Example 2 (Bitcoin Daily)

Area of resistance

Ascending triangle
buildup

This bitcoin example is similar to the USDCNH example, so I won't go into much details. However, I want you to pay attention to the buildup that's formed. Unlike the earlier example where the buildup resembled a "box," this buildup has a series of higher lows coming into resistance (also known as an ascending triangle).

Again, this is a sign of strength because it shows you that buyers are willing to buy at higher prices, and there's a lack of selling pressure to push the price lower. Your stop loss can go 1 ATR below the previous swing low or below the trendline (which you can connect from the lows).

Figure 6.10 – MBEE Formula Example 3 (USD/CAD Daily)

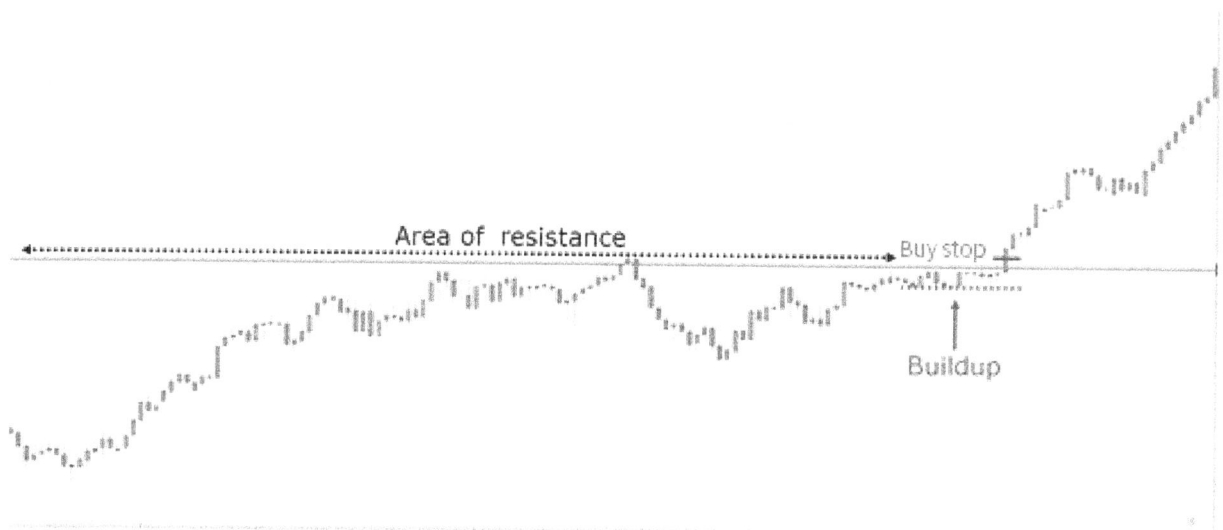

Area of resistance

Buy stop

Buildup

USDCAD is in an advancing stage (market structure). Now, you could argue this is a potential distribution stage, and you wouldn't be wrong either. As you can see, price action trading can be subjective, and different traders can interpret the markets differently. But why I'm bullish is because the uptrend is intact, and there's a buildup formed at resistance (which is a sign of strength).

However, I don't want to jump into the trade too early just because I'm bullish—the breakout might not occur. Instead, I'll place a buy stop order above the highs. If it's triggered, I'm long (or else, I'm on the sidelines). The key here is to trade what you see, not what you think (no matter how confident you are).

Now, you might be thinking, "Is there a variation of the MBEE formula?" Of course! In the earlier examples, the buildup occurs before the breakout. But there are times when the buildup forms *after* the breakout. Here's what I mean:

Figure 6.11 – MBEE Formula Example 4 (EUR/USD Daily)

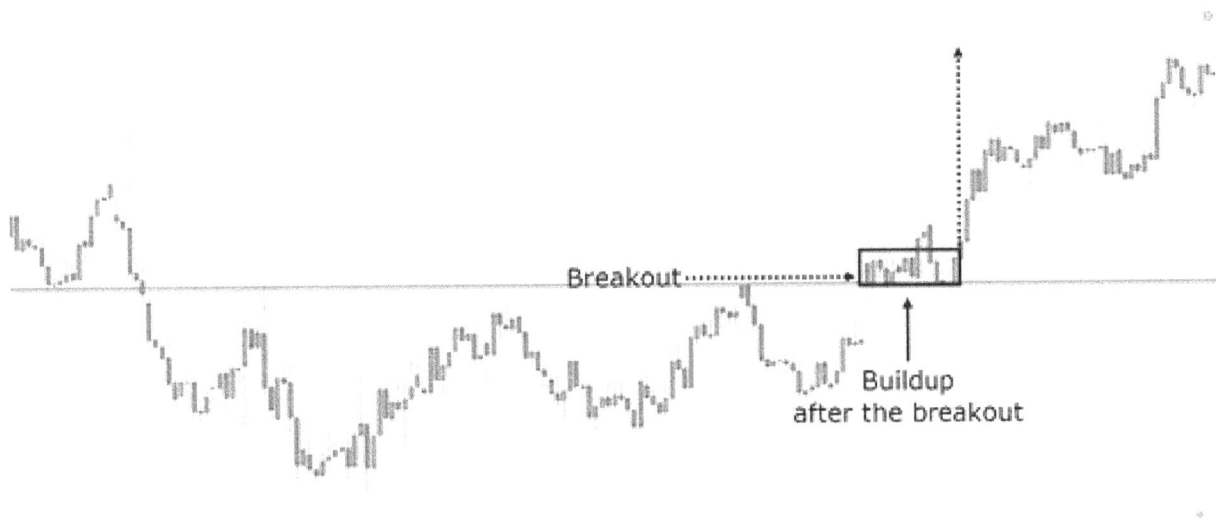

BONUS TIPS (MBEE FORMULA)

1. Don't trade into "traffic"

Let me ask you, when you need to get to your destination in the fastest possible time, do you use the highway with less traffic or the smaller roads with high traffic? It's a no-brainer: You use the highway.

It's the same for trading. When you place a trade, you want as little "traffic" as possible. So if you're selling breakdowns, you don't want to sell into support since that's where buying pressure is lurking. Here's an example:

Figure 6.12 – Avoid selling into support (EUR/GBP Daily)

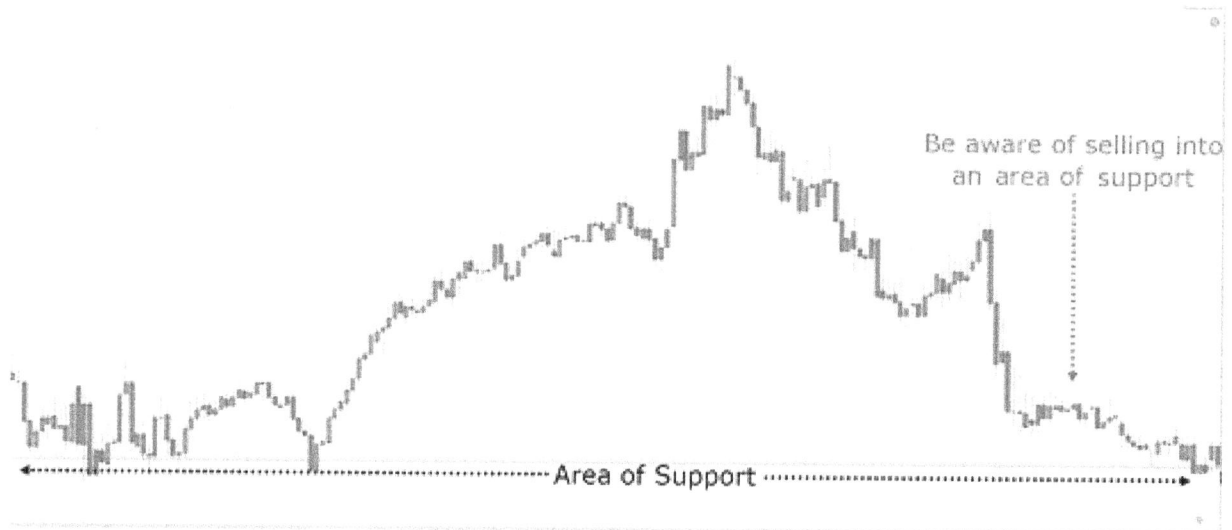

Even though there's a buildup formed on EURGBP, I would avoid shorting this market because a little below my entry point, there's an area of support (around 0.8500) where buying pressure could step in and push the price higher.

So if your stop loss is 1 ATR above the highs of the buildup, and your target profit is at support, this means you're risking $1 to make $0.3—a poor risk-to-reward ratio. Remember, don't trade into "traffic." Instead, find trading setups with little-or-no "traffic" so the price can quickly move from one area to the next.

2. Let the 20-period moving average (MA) be your guide

One of the struggles I used to face when identifying buildups was wondering how long they should be. Five candles? Ten candles? Twenty candles? I didn't have a definite answer because it depends on the context of the markets, so I looked through my past trades and found something important. I realized the best buildup occurs when it has enough time to "digest" the recent move.

So if you're looking for a bullish buildup, you'll notice the 20-period moving average (MA) has caught up with the lows of the buildup—and that's when the market is ready to break out. Here's what I mean:

Figure 6.13 – Let the 20-period moving average "catch up" with the buildup (GBP/JPY Daily)

In addition, your stop loss is even more "protected" since it's 1 ATR below the lows of the buildup, which coincides with the 20 MA. Nice!

3. The tighter the buildup, the better

You can think of a buildup as the market storing "potential" energy for the move that's going to happen later. So the tighter the buildup, the more "potential" energy is stored up for release—and the stronger the breakout. Also, you want to avoid loose buildup which looks like a range market with obvious swing highs and lows. Why?

There are two reasons for this: 1) When the buildup is loose, your stop loss is larger, which reduces your risk-to-reward ratio on the trade. 2) If you're in a long trade, the highs of a loose buildup are where selling pressure is lurking (since it's resistance on the lower time frame), and that's an obstacle you have to overcome.

THE DERR FORMULA

The DERR formula is a process that can transform your trading even if you've been losing for years or breaking even for the longest time. DERR stands for develop your trading plan, execute, record, and review.

A trading plan is a set of guidelines that define your trading. This reduces subjectivity in your trading, prepares you for the worst-case scenario, and allows you to be a consistent trader. This is powerful, right? So how do you develop a trading plan? Well, it needs to answer these six questions:

What is your time frame?

This depends on the amount of time you can commit to trading. If you can set aside 10 hours a day for trading, then trading the lower time frames is possible. But if you have a full-time job and can't spend the whole day watching the markets, then consider trading the daily or weekly time frame.

What markets are you trading?

If, for example, you want to trade stocks, what type of stocks will you trade? They could be the large-cap, mid-cap, or small-cap. Or, if you are going to trade forex, which currency pairs will you focus on? You must define the markets to trade or you'll be all over the place (trying to "shoot" anything that moves).

What are the conditions of your trading setup?

For example, if you trade breakouts, how will you enter a breakout? You might go for the 50-day highs, the 200-day highs, the highest close over the last 100 days, etc. Also, are there any other conditions that must occur for you to trade the breakout? For example, your condition might be that you only trade when the market is in an uptrend, or a low volatility environment, etc.

How will you exit your trade if you're wrong?

You should set your stop loss at a level that invalidates your trading setup. For example, if you trade a breakout, then what level on the chart would the price have to hit to signal to you that the breakout has failed? That's where you set your stop loss.

How will you exit your trade if you're right?

This depends on your goals. Are you trying to capture a swing or ride a trend? Once you decide this, you can use the appropriate technique. If you want to ride a trend, then you must trail your stop loss. Alternatively, if you want to capture a swing, you must have a fixed target profit.

How much do you risk per trade?

Recall that if your drawdown gets too deep, it will be nearly impossible to get back up (since the math is against you). So the key is to risk a fraction of your capital on every trade (my suggestion is not to risk more than 1% of your account).

How many units do you trade?

Once you've defined your entry point, stop loss, and the amount you want to risk, then you can calculate the correct position size to trade. Now, you don't have to calculate it manually because you can use a position size calculator. You can find one on Google or get one here:

priceactiontradingsecrets.com/bonus

Let me give you a template you can use for your trading plan. Here's an example:

If I'm trading, then I'll focus on the Russell 1000 stocks and on the daily time frame (markets traded and time frame).

If the price is above the 200-day moving average and makes a 200-day high, then I'll go long on the next candle's open (conditions of your trading setup).

If my entry is triggered, then I'll have a trailing stop loss of 20% from the highs (exit).

If I get stopped out of the trade, then my loss will not be more than 1% of my capital (risk management).

Execute

Next, you'll execute your trades according to your trading plan. After doing this, one of five things can happen:

14. Breakeven trades.
15. Small wins.
16. Small losses.

17. Big wins.

18. Big losses.

The key thing here is to eliminate big losses from your trading (with proper risk management). If you can do this, profitable trading is closer than you think.

If you recall, in the short-run your trading results are random (due to the law of large numbers) and in the long run, they will gravitate towards the systems' expectancy. So don't abandon your trading strategy after a few losing trades because the results don't mean a thing. Instead, you want to execute the same setup at least 100 times before you can come up with a conclusion to whether your trading strategy works or not. Moving on…

Record

I know this isn't exciting stuff, but you must record your trades if you want to become the best price action trader you can be. This is what separates the pros from the amateur traders, so are you ready to be a pro? If so, here are the metrics you must record for every trade:

Date: Date you entered your trade.

Time frame: Time frame you entered on.

Set up: The type of trade (it could be a breakout, reversal, trend trading, etc.)

Market: Markets you're trading.

Price in: Price you entered.

Price out: Price you exited.

Stop loss: Price at which you'll exit when you're wrong.

Profit and loss in R: What's the risk-to-reward ratio on the trade? (If you risked $5 and made $10, then it's a gain of 2R.)

Once you've recorded your metrics, you might want to screen capture the charts so you'll know what it looked like before and after the trade (this is useful for doing your trade review, as I'll explain later).

You want to save three types of charts for every trade:

1. Chart of the higher time frame.

2. Chart of the entry time frame.

3. Chart after the trade is completed.

Chart of the higher time frame

This chart is one time frame above your entry time frame. For example, if you entered on the daily time frame, your higher time frame would be the weekly. The purpose of saving charts that show the higher time frame is so that you'll know where you are in the big picture. You want to answer questions like *What's the trend? What's the market structure. Where are the areas of value?* And so on.

Chart of the entry time frame

This is the chart you used to make your buy/sell decisions. For this, you want to identify the trading setup and mark your entry and stop loss.

Chart after the trade is completed

Finally, you'll want to save the chart after the trade is completed. You'll want to answer questions, like *What was your profit or loss in terms of R? Did you follow your trading plan? If you broke your rules, why did this happen?*

Review

After you execute and record your trades (at least 100 of them), you can review them to see if you have an edge in the markets. Generally, if your trading account is green after 100 trades, chances are you have an edge in the markets. But to break it down further, here's a formula you can use:

*Expectancy = (Winning % * Average win) – (Losing % * Average loss) – (Commission + Slippage)*

Here's an example, let's say your strategy has:

*   A 50% winning rate.

*   A 50% losing rate.

- Average win of $1000.

- Average loss of $500.

- Average commission and slippage of $10.

Plug these into the formula, and you get:

Expectancy = (0.5 * 1000) – (0.5 * 500) – (10)

= $240

If you get a positive expectancy, it means your trading strategy has an edge in the markets. Now you're probably wondering, "But what does the number mean?" In our earlier example, it means you'll earn an average of $240 per trade in the long run. But what if you get a negative expectancy? What now? Well, that's where your trading journal comes into play. I'll explain.

Identify patterns that lead to your winners

Because you recorded and captured screen shots of your trades, you can identify the common patterns that lead to your winners—and focus on making similar trades. For example, one of my "aha" moments came when I realized that most of my successful breakout trades occurred after a buildup was formed. So what did I do? I focused on trading breakouts with a buildup. If there's no buildup, then there are no breakout trades for me.

Identify patterns that lead to your losses

Likewise, you can look at your losses and identify common patterns that lead to these losses—and avoid making the same kinds of trades. This will reduce your losses and improve your overall profitability.

Remove large losses

You can trade with an edge and follow your trading plan 95% of the time—and still lose money. Why? This happens because for the remaining 5% of the time, you break your rules and incur huge losses that erode all your profits.

If that sounds like you, then ask yourself why you do this. Is it because of the fear of losing, the fear of missing out, or the fear of being wrong? Be honest with yourself. Then write down the steps you'll take to prevent it from happening again—and follow them.

Ultimately, if you want to improve your trading, you must review your trades. That's only possible if you have a trading plan that you execute and record consistently—otherwise known as the DERR formula.

"If you can't measure it, you can't improve it." — Peter Drucker.

You can see how everything comes together using the three formulas I've taught you. The MAEE and MBEE formulas allow you to develop your own trading strategies to trade reversals and breakouts. And finally, the DERR formula helps you to constantly review and improve your trading results. But remember, these are simply formulas to guide your responses, they're not cast in stone. So feel free to tweak them and modify them to suit your own needs. Cool?

SUMMARY

- The MAEE formula helps you develop a reversal trading strategy.

- The MBEE formula helps you develop a breakout trading strategy.

- The DERR formula allows you to be consistent in your trading so you can review and improve your trading results.

ADVANCED PRICE ACTION TRADING TECHNIQUES THAT NOBODY TELLS YOU

At this stage, you're ready to go back into the "wild" and figure things out on your own. However, I don't want to leave you only semi-equipped to fight the war. I want to provide the best so you can survive and have the tools you need to win the war. So here are nine price action trading techniques I've learned over the years that will take your price action trading skills to the next level.

PRE-BREAKOUT TECHNIQUE: HOW TO ENTER A BREAKOUT BEFORE THE BREAKOUT

I discovered this technique by accident. Here's a quick story. A few years back, as I was reviewing my breakout trades, I wondered to myself, "How can I enter a breakout before it occurs?" The next thing I knew, I was looking at the lower time frame and something caught my attention!

I realized that when the market is forming a buildup, there's an opportunity to time your entry on the lower time frame. In other words, when the price is forming a buildup, you can go down to a lower time frame and look for price rejection at the lows of the buildup (which is a swing low or support on the lower time frame).

And if there's a price rejection in the lows of a buildup, you can go long on the next candle in the hope that the price will break out of consolidation higher. Here's an example:

Figure 7.1 – A buildup (Brent Crude Oil Weekly)

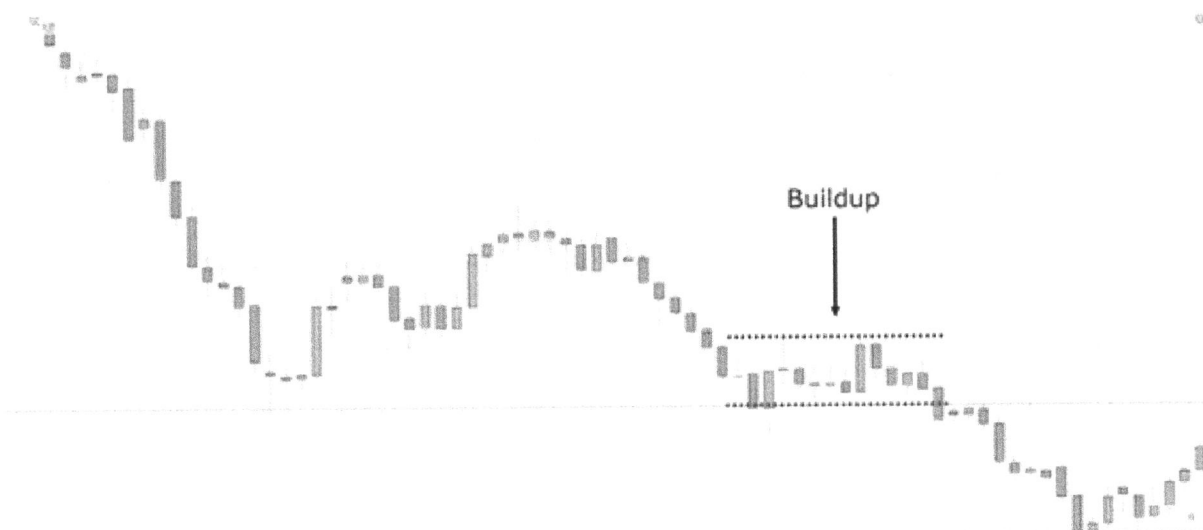

Figure 7.2 – Bearish price rejection (Brent Crude Oil Daily)

If you think about it, this is actually the MAEE formula using multiple time frame analysis. And since the higher time frame is forming a buildup, you want to adopt a trailing stop loss technique that allows you to capture the potential breakout.

Also, I've prepared a bonus training to share more details about this pre-breakout technique. You can get it here: priceactiontradingsecrets.com/bonus

NOT ALL TRENDS ARE CREATED EQUAL. HERE'S WHAT YOU MUST KNOW...

You know that an uptrend consists of higher highs and lows, right? But here's the thing. Not all trends are the same even though they have higher highs and lows. Why? Because it's the depth of the pullback that matters. So to take things a step further, you can classify trends into one of three types: strong trends, healthy trends, and weak trends. Let's examine each of these.

In a strong uptrend, the pullback is shallow (not more than 38% retracement), and the price finds support around the 20-period moving average. Because the pullback is shallow, it's difficult to time your entry on the pullback because the price would quickly reverse higher if you were "slow." Thus, it's easier to trade breakouts in a strong trending market. Here's an example:

Figure 7.3 – In a strong trend, you can look to trade the breakout (USD/ZAR Weekly)

In a strong trend, you can look to buy the breakout of the swing high

20 MA

Still, if you want to trade the pullback, my suggestion is to use the pre-breakout technique that you learned earlier.

Next…

In a downtrend uptrend, the pullback is obvious (not more than 50% retracement), and the price finds resistance around the 50-period moving average. Since this pullback is deeper, you've got enough time to time your entry on the pullback, possibly looking for a "bounce" near the 50-period moving average. Also, in a healthy trend, the price tends to re-test previous support, which now becomes resistance (near the 50-period moving average). Here's what I mean:

Figure 7.4 – In a healthy trend, you can look to trade the pullback around the 50-period moving average (EUR/JPY Daily)

In a healthy trend, you can look to trade
the pullback towards the 50 MA

50 MA

Finally, a weak downtrend has deep pullbacks (at least 62% retracement) and the price finds buying pressure around the 200-period moving average. In a market condition like this, you don't want to buy breakouts because you'll likely get stopped out on the pullback. Instead, you can time your entries on the pullback towards the 200-period moving average or at resistance. Let me give you an example:

Figure 7.5 – In a weak trend, you can look to trade the pullback around the 200-period moving average (AUD/JPY Daily)

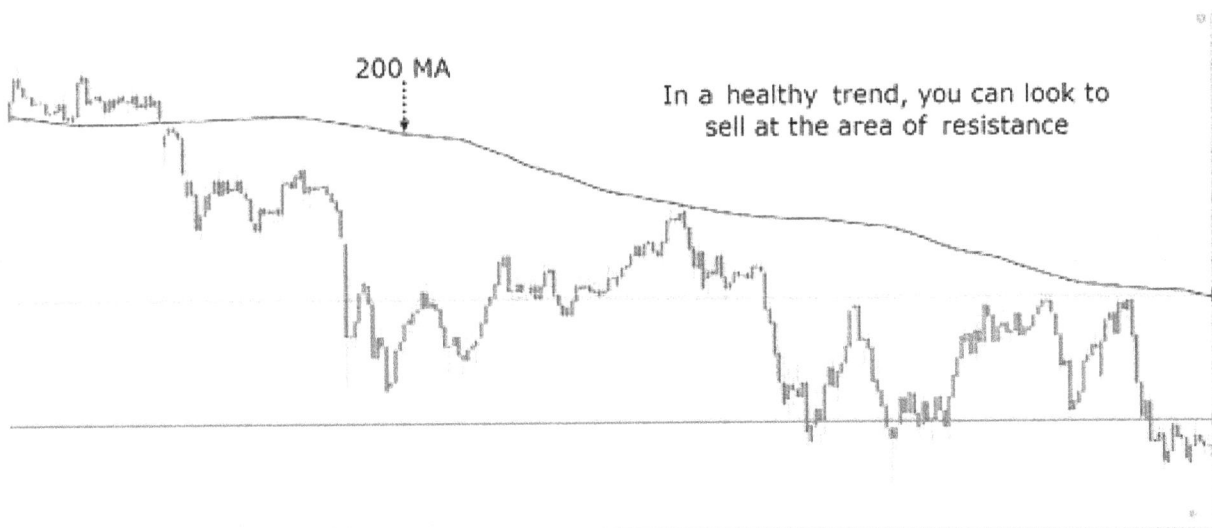

200 MA

In a healthy trend, you can look to
sell at the area of resistance

DON'T TRADE IN THE DIRECTION OF THE TREND WHEN THE

PRICE IS "OVERSTRETCHED"

When the market is trending, it tends to pull back towards the mean. For example, in a healthy uptrend, the price tends to pull back towards the 50-period moving average (MA). So you want to look for buying opportunities when the price is near the 50 MA, not when it's far from it. Why?

If you buy when the price is far above the 50 MA, your stop loss must be below the 50 MA to invalidate your trading setup—and that's a wide stop loss that offers a poor risk-to-reward ratio.

On the other hand, if your stop loss is above the 50 MA, you'll likely get stopped out on the pullback even though the uptrend is still intact. Here's what I mean…

Figure 7.6 – Avoid trading when the price is far away from the respected moving average (T-Bond Daily)

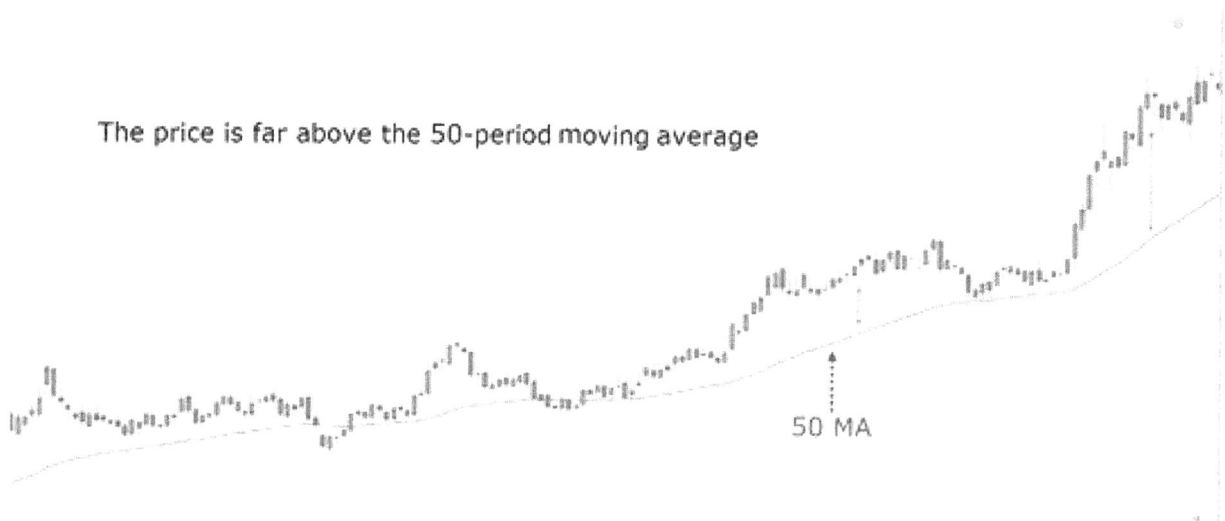

The price is far above the 50-period moving average

50 MA

In this case, a better approach would be to buy near the 50 MA since you have a tighter stop loss, which improves your risk-to-reward ratio. And even if you get stopped out, this will happen because your trading setup is invalidated and not due to some random noise in the markets.

HOW TO IDENTIFY HIDDEN STRENGTH AND WEAKNESS IN THE MARKETS

As you know, the market doesn't go up in a straight line. Instead, there's an ebb and flow to it—it goes up, makes a pullback, then continues higher, and so on. And if you take things a step further, you can classify this "up-and-down" pattern as a trending move and a retracement move.

A trending move is the "stronger" leg of the trend. You'll notice the body and range of the candles are larger—and it trades in the direction of the trend. Here's an example:

Figure 7.7 – Trending move (EUR/USD 4-hour)

On the other hand, a retracement move is the "weaker" leg of the trend. You'll notice that both the body and the range of candles are smaller—and it trades against the direction of the trend. Here's what I mean:

Figure 7.8 – Retracement move (EUR/USD 4-hour)

So why am I sharing this? Simple. In a normal trend, you'd expect a trending move followed by a retracement move. But when the trend weakens, you'll notice that the range of the retracement moves gets larger (in contrast to the smaller ones you usually see). And when you combine this with market structure and area of value, you can pinpoint market turning points with accuracy. Here's an example:

NZD/CAD Daily:

In the daily time frame, the price is a resistance area and has the confluence of a downward trendline. The price could reverse lower, so let's look for a shorting opportunity on the lower time frame…

Figue 7.9 – The price is at resistance (NZD/CAD Daily)

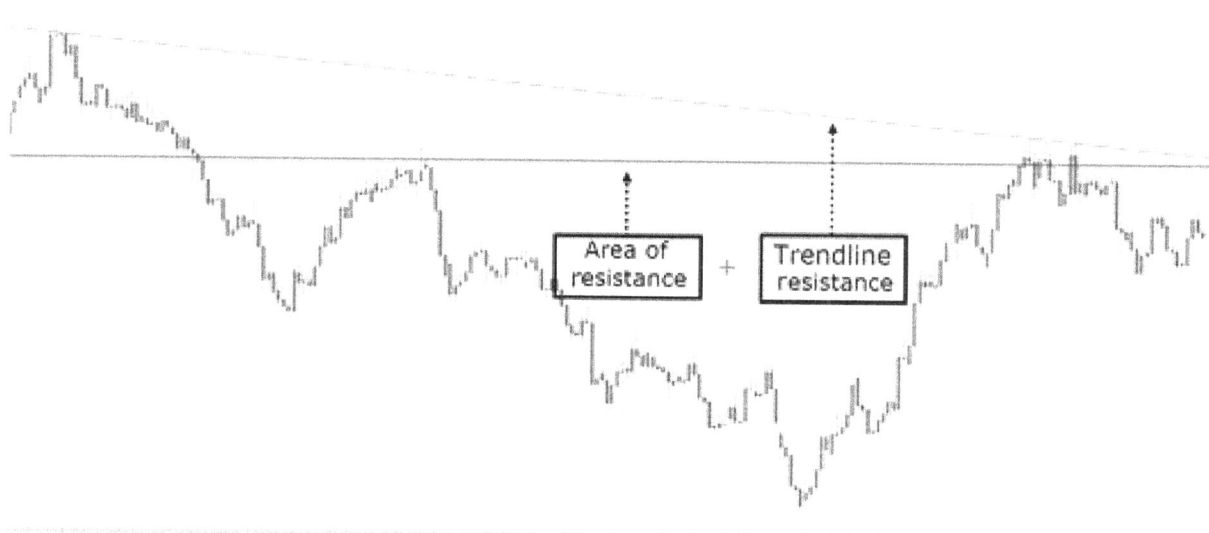

NZD/CAD 8-hour:

In the 8-hour time frame, the selling pressure is coming in: You'll notice the candles of the retracement moves getting bigger (a sign of strength from the sellers). Also, the buying pressure is becoming weak since the candles of the trending move are getting smaller. One possible entry technique is to go short when the price breaks and closes below support:

Figure 7.10 – Retracement moves getting larger (NZD/CAD 8-hour)

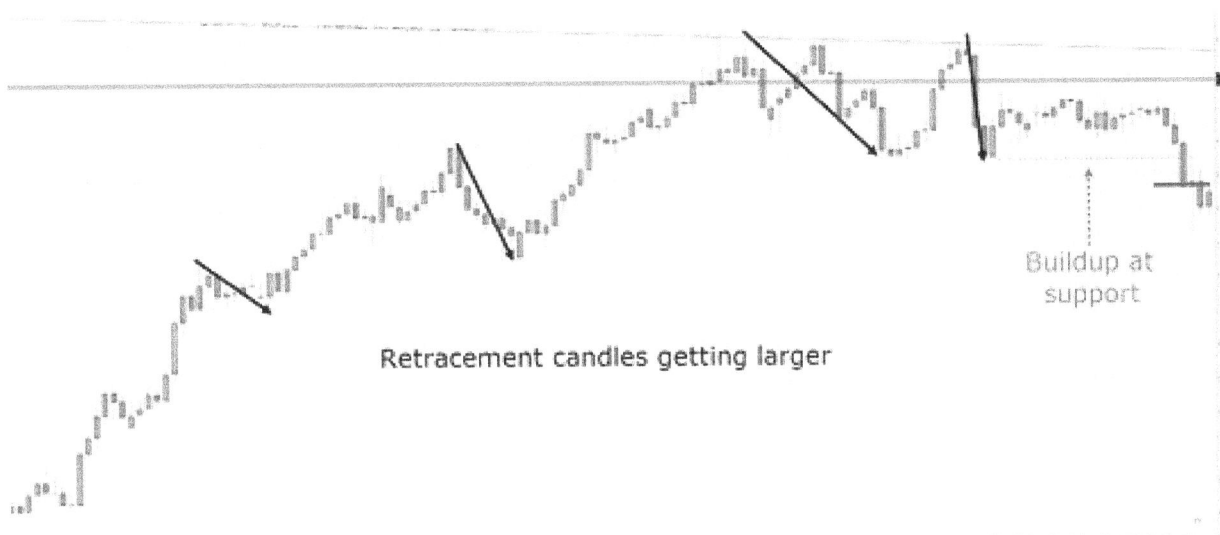

Retracement candles getting larger

Buildup at support

Can you see how all the different techniques you've learned are coming together now?

HOW TO TELL WHEN THE MARKET IS EXHAUSTED AND ABOUT TO REVERSE

Every day when the market opens, it has a finite amount of "energy" to move before it exhausts itself (kind of like a car with a tank of fuel). But the question is, how do you know when the market is exhausted and unlikely to move further? Well, that's where the average true range (ATR) indicator comes into play.

The ATR indicator measures volatility in the markets. So if a 20-period ATR (in the daily time frame) is 100 pips, this means the market has moved an average of 100 pips/day over the last 20 days.

This doesn't mean the market will reverse after moving 100 pips for the day because it can "stretch" further than that. But it sets the boundary for how much the market can potentially move in a given day. And when you combine this technique with support and resistance, market structure, candlestick patterns, etc., it can help you filter for high probability reversal trades.

NOT ALL MARKETS ARE CREATED EQUAL, HERE'S WHY...

If you've read most types of trading materials, they'll tell you the market trends 30% of the time. However, this isn't true. Let me prove it to you...

I applied a simple trend-following system to different markets (credit to Andrea Unger for sharing this in the book *Trading Mentors: Learn Timeless Strategies and Best Practices from Successful Traders*). Here's how it works…

19. Buy the breakout of previous day's high.

20. Hold the long position until the price hits the previous day's low, and go short.

21. Hold the short position until the price breaks above the previous day's high, and go long.

22. Rinse and repeat.

    If you think about it, this is a simple trend-following system that should make you money when a market exhibits trending behavior, and it should lose you money if a market exhibits mean-reverting behavior.

    Next, I applied this system to two markets, GBP/USD and AUD/CAD. Here are the results:

    Figure 7.11 – GBP/USD equity curve in an uptrend when a trend-following approach is used

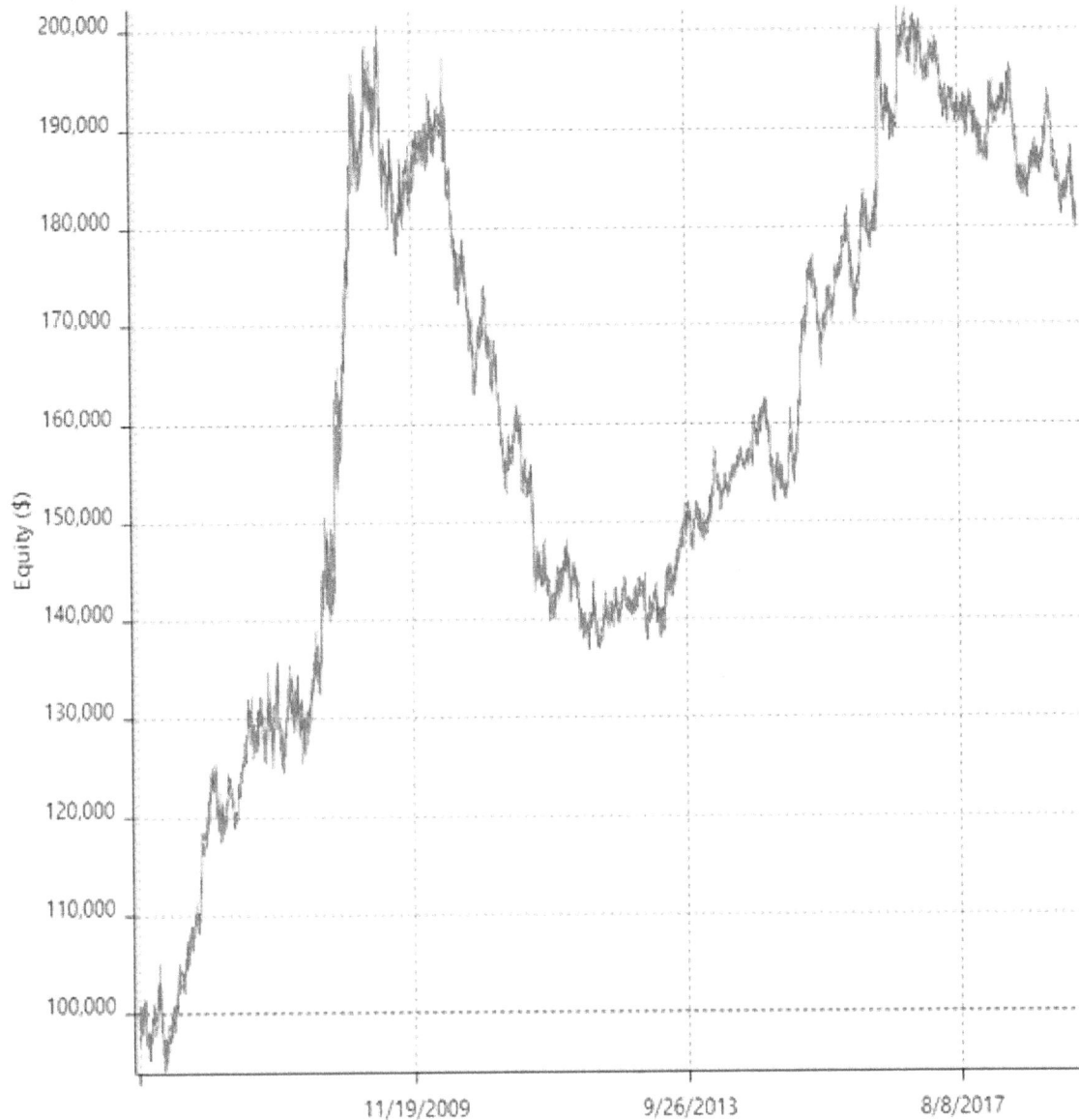

You can see an equity curve that's moving higher. This tells you GBP/USD is a trending market because it makes money when you use a trend-following approach to trade it.

Figure 7.12 – AUD/CAD equity curve showing new lows when a trend-following approach is used

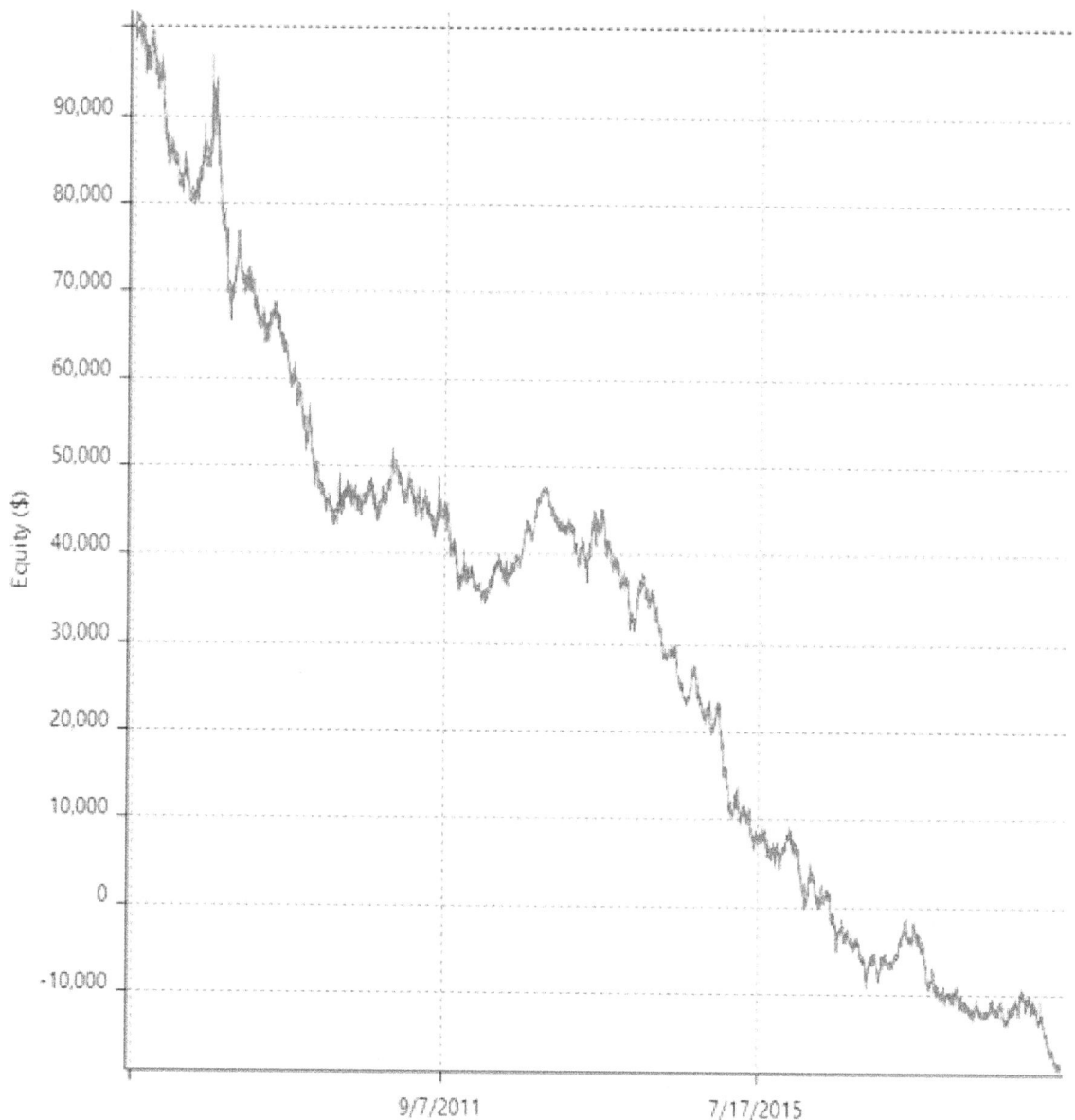

Now you can see an equity curve that's heading lower. Clearly, AUD/CAD is a mean-reverting market because it loses money when a trend-following approach is traded on it.

You can do this test on your own to find out which markets have trending or mean-reverting behavior (this concept can also be applied to the weekly time frame). So what can you do with this insight? One way is to use different trade management for different market behavior.

For example, if you know GBP/USD has shown trending behavior in the daily time frame, then you'll want to consider trailing your stop loss for this market since you have a better chance of riding a trend. And for AUD/CAD, you can have a fixed target profit at the previous day's high/low since it tends to reverse around that level. Make sense?

HOW TO MANAGE YOUR TRADES LIKE A PRO USING HIGHER TIME FRAME ANALYSIS

As you grow as a trader, you'll realize different trade management techniques are better suited for different market conditions. For example, let's say you used the MAEE formula and entered a long trade at support (on the daily time frame). How do you know whether to capture a swing, ride a trend, or adopt a hybrid approach?

This is where you can look at the higher time frame for guidance. Imagine the higher time frame is in a strong uptrend. What would you do? Well, you can consider holding the trade longer since the uptrend is strong with shallow pullbacks, which makes it easy to ride the trend.

But what if the higher time frame is in a potential distribution stage? Then you'll want to consider exiting your position at the nearest swing high before the market reverses lower.

Or what if the market is in a potential accumulation stage? Well, you can sell half of your position at resistance and hold the remaining to see if the price can break out of resistance. *If* it does, great! You've still got half your position to ride the new uptrend. But if it doesn't, your losses are minimized because you've exited half your position at a profit.

Now, this can get complex and messy if you don't know what you're doing. So my suggestion is to keep things simple at the start. When you level up as a trader, you can consider more advanced trade management techniques like this one.

HOW TO TELL WHEN THE MARKET IS ABOUT TO MAKE A BIG MOVE

If you look at most charts, you'll realize the volatility of the market is always changing. It can move from a period of low volatility to a period of high volatility and vice versa. This means when the market is quiet, you should expect something big to happen soon. And if the market is moving crazily, expect it to get quiet soon.

Here's an example:

Figure 7.13 – The market moves from a period of high volatility to low volatility (and vice versa)

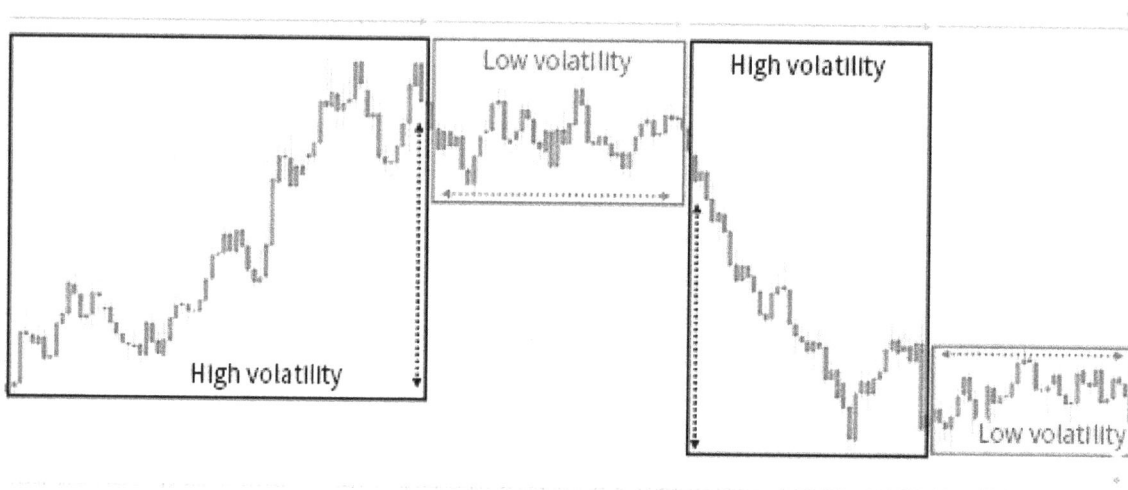

Newbie price action traders love to trade high-volatility markets because that's where the excitement is. But the problem with a high volatility environment is that your stop loss needs to be wider to take into account the "noise" in the market—and this offers a poor risk-to-reward ratio. Also, high volatility occurs when the market is about to enter a low volatility environment, so this is where they'll get "stuck" in their trades.

In contrast, professional price action traders love entering low-volatility environments. Your stop loss is tighter, thus allowing you to put on a larger position size (while risking the same amount). And if volatility expands in your favor, it offers a favorable risk-to-reward ratio (possibly 1:5 or more).

You're probably wondering, "How do I find trades in a low volatility market environment?" Well, you can apply the MBEE formula or the pre-breakout technique that you learned earlier. As you can see, a lot of the stuff you're learning here builds on the concepts you learned earlier. So if you're unsure, spend some time revisiting the earlier chapters. Don't rush into things because trading is a marathon, not a sprint.

AT THIS POINT...

You've learned nine advanced price action trading techniques that will help you better time your entries and exits. In the next section, I want to share a few trading examples based on the concepts you've learned. This will give you better insights into my thought processes, including what I look for in a trade and why I choose to avoid certain setups.

SUMMARY

- The pre-breakout technique allows you to enter a breakout before it occurs by identifying price rejection (at support or swing low) on the lower time frame.

- There are three categories of trends: strong trends, healthy trends, and weak trends.

- You want to avoid trading in the direction of the trend when the price is far from the mean.

- Pay attention to the trending and retracement moves because this gives you clues to the strength and weakness in the markets.

- The average true range (ATR) gives you an idea of how much the market can potentially move in a day.

- Not all markets are the same. Some will exhibit trending behavior while others will exhibit mean-reverting behavior.

- You can refer to the market structure on the higher time frame to help you better manage your trades (to determine whether to capture a swing, ride a trend, or adopt a hybrid approach).

- The market moves in volatility cycles, from periods of low volatility to periods of high volatility (and vice versa).

TRADING EXAMPLES

When I was in the army, I met an interesting guy named James during my demolition course. During the course, we had to pass both a theory and a practical exam before we could qualify as demolition men.

At that time, my impression was that if you did well on your theory test, then your practical test should be a breeze. So when James did badly on his theory test, I thought his practical test would be a disaster. Boy, was I wrong. James came out on top for his practical test even though his theory was crap.

That's when I realized different people have different modes of learning. And for most people, the best way to learn is through practical examples so they can see how everything comes together. So here's how it works...

I'll break down the thought process behind each trade, discuss my entries, stop losses, and exits. I won't reveal the outcome of each trade because it's not important (and it's random). Now, I don't expect you to trade like me, so take what's useful to you, ditch what's irrelevant, and use this to develop your own trading plan. Ready? Then let's kick things off with breakout trades…

Figure 8.1 – Trading example 1: breakout (NZD/JPY Daily)

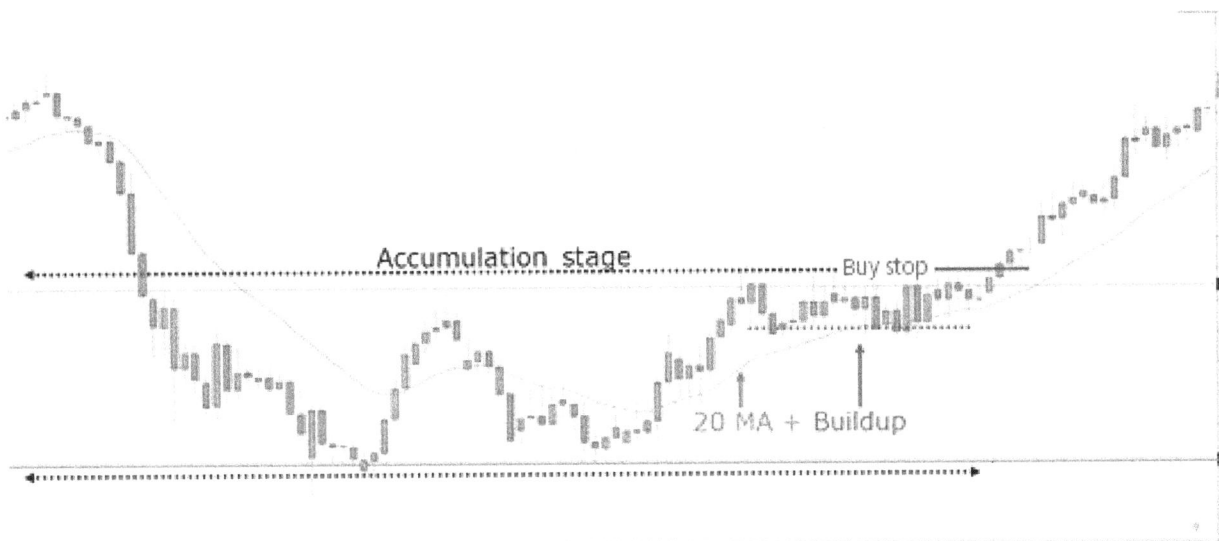

NZDJPY is in a potential accumulation stage, and it's approaching resistance at 70.00. You can see a series of higher lows approaching resistance—and a buildup formed right now. This is a sign of strength because it tells me the buyers are willing to buy at higher prices—even at resistance. Also, if you overlay the 20 MA, you'll notice it has caught up with the lows of a buildup, which signals that the market is getting ready to break out.

So my plan is to have a buy stop order placed above the highs of resistance and have a stop loss of 1 ATR below the lows of the buildup. Now, if the breakout is real, this could transit into stage two, the advancing stage, and I want to ride the trend as long as it lasts. Thus, I'll adopt a trailing stop loss of 3 ATR if the trade moves in my favor (if you need a video explanation of how to use the ATR indicator to trail your stop loss, you can get it at priceactiontradingsecrets.com/bonus).

I hope you've realized this is actually the MBEE formula you learned earlier. The only difference is that we're doing this example as close to "real-time" as possible. So use this formula and ask yourself how else you could tweak this for your own needs.

Figure 8.2 – Trading example 2: breakout (EUR/NZD Daily)

EURNZD is in a range market. This isn't an accumulation or distribution stage because if you zoom out, the market is still in a range. Nevertheless, there's still a trading opportunity because the market broke below support and is now forming a buildup at previous support, which has now become resistance. Again, if you overlay the 20MA, you'll notice it has caught up with the highs of the buildup, signaling that the market could make a move soon.

My plan is to place a sell stop order below the lows of the buildup and have a stop loss of 1 ATR above the highs of the buildup. If you're looking to ride a trend, you can use a trailing stop. Alternatively, if you want to capture a swing, 1.6600 is an area where you'll want to consider taking profits because it's a major swing low, and buying pressure could step in.

Now, a common question I get is "Rayner, why do you set your stop loss 1 ATR above the highs of a buildup. Why not 0.5 ATR or 2 ATR?" Yes, you could do that. But remember, the idea is to give your stop loss "room to breathe" so you don't get stopped out by a sudden spike that takes out the highs. So the amount of "breathing room" you'll want to give it is determined by the multiple of your ATR. The higher your multiple, the larger your stop loss (and vice versa).

Don't bother trying to figure out the best parameter, the best moving average, the best trailing stop loss, the best settings, or any other best choice because there's no best out there. Instead, work on understanding the concept behind what you're trying to achieve, and then use the appropriate tools to move towards that. This is the way you should approach trading.

Figure 8.3 – Trading example 3: breakout (Bitcoin Daily)

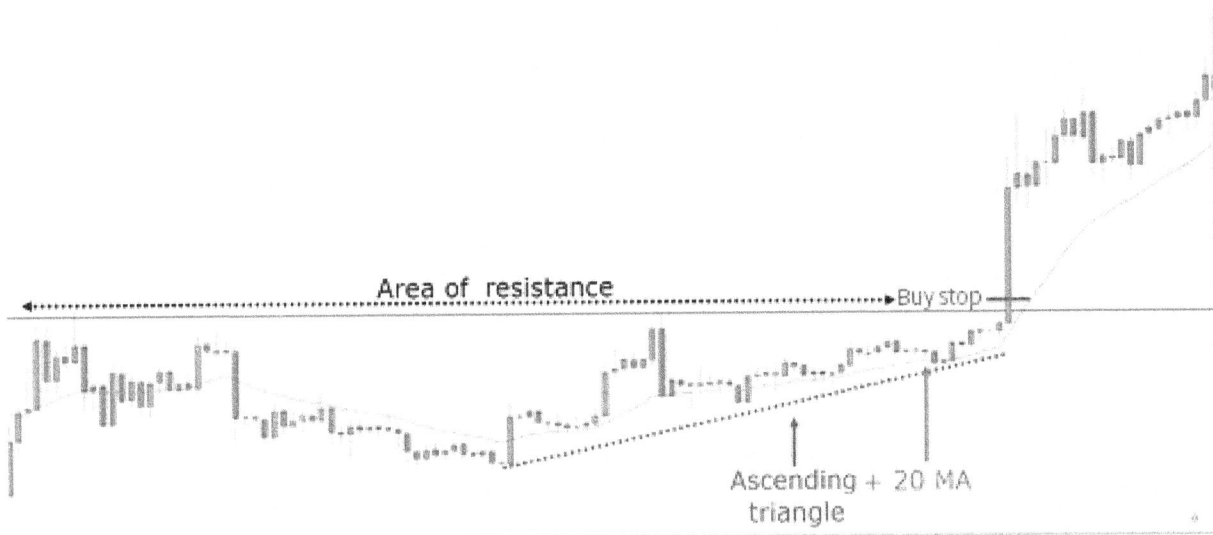

Bitcoin is in an accumulation stage, and it's near resistance at $4200. You can see a series of higher lows as it moves into resistance (also known as an ascending triangle), which is a sign of strength because buyers are willing to buy at high prices. And if you overlay this chart with the 20 MA, you'll see it has come into contact with the price and is "supporting" it higher into resistance.

The plan is simple. I'm looking to place a buy stop order above the highs of resistance and have my stop loss set 1 ATR below the previous minor swing low. If the price moves in my favor, I'll use 3 ATR to trail my stop loss. In this type of market condition, I always ride the trend with a trailing stop loss because the transition from accumulation to the advancing stage is where new trends are born.

Next, we'll discuss reversal trades.

Figure 8.4 – Trading example 4: reversal (EUR/CAD Daily)

EURCAD is in a declining stage with a series of lower highs and lows. Right now, the price made a swing into resistance, followed by a bearish engulfing pattern. This is a rejection of higher prices and buyers who bought at the breakout of resistance are now in the red.

Since this market is in a downtrend and at resistance (area of value), I intend to short this market on the next candle's open. My stop loss is 1 ATR above the bearish engulfing pattern. As for target profit, you can choose the nearest swing low at 1.4550 or the one that is further away at 1.4450 (I suggest having your target profit a few pips above the swing low because the price might not re-test the exact level).

In terms of trade management, you can exit half of your position at target one and the remaining half at target two. Of course, you can adjust how much you want to exit at target one or two. Generally, however, you'll want to keep at least 50% of your position for target two, or else the gains will not be meaningful.

One last thing, I'd classify this as a weak trend. And in this type of market condition, I'd prefer to capture one swing, the reason being that in a weak trend, the pullback is steep and having a trailing stop loss would erode most of my open profits. Thus, I'd go with capturing a swing instead.

Figure 8.5 – Trading example 5: reversal (WTI Daily)

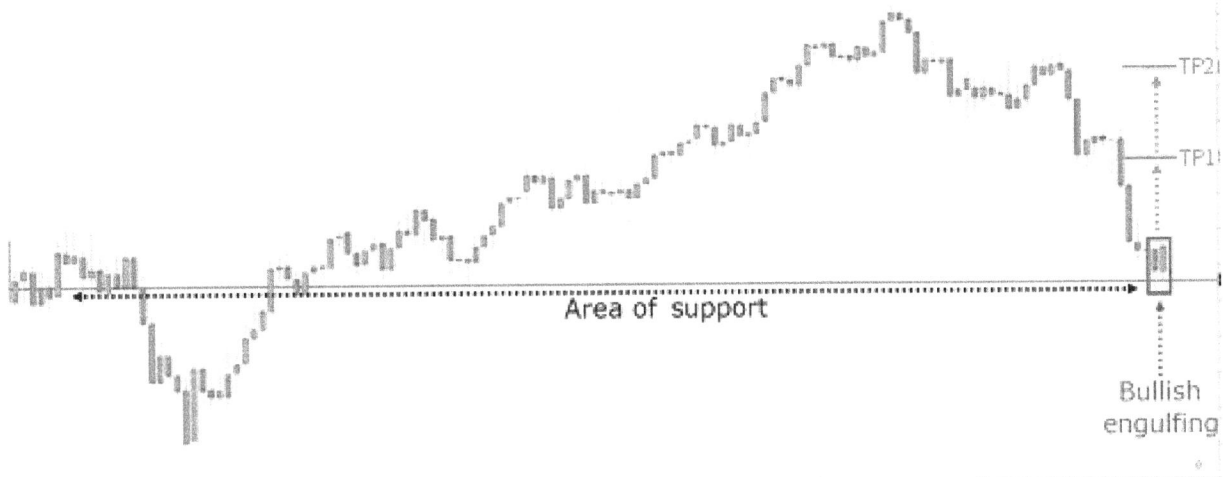

WTI (Western Texas Oil) is in a range market, and the price made a power move into support. Next, the price traded below support at 51.15, only to make a sudden reversal—closing near the high of the day. At this point, traders who short the breakdown (of support) are in the red.

To profit from this group of trapped traders, my plan is to go long on the next candle's open with a stop loss 1 ATR below the low. As for target profit, I'm looking at 58.00 and 63.00 because that's where selling pressure could step in.

Now, let's talk a little bit about trade management. It's easy to have your entries, stop loss, and target profit defined. But what if the price moves in your favor, let's say to 57.5—just shy of your first target—and it starts to reverse lower. What would you do?

Do you hold onto your trade until it hits your stop loss? Or do you shift your stop loss to break even? Or do you exit part of your position? Clearly, there are no right or wrong answers, but you must take this into consideration (something most traders neglect).

Figure 8.6 – Trading example 6: reversal (GBP/USD Daily)

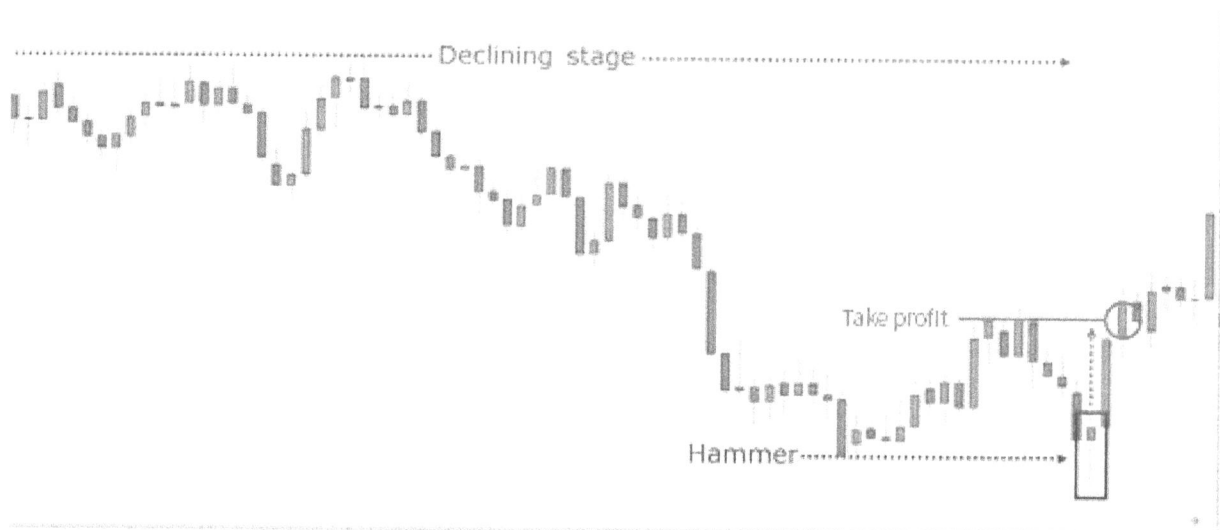

GBPUSD is in a declining stage, also known as a downtrend. Next, the price made a clean move into the swing low, only to be rejected strongly as the price closed higher (and formed a bullish hammer). Clearly, the traders who shorted the breakdown are in the red now.

My plan is to go long on the next candle's open with a stop loss of 1 ATR below the low of the candle. As for target profit, I'll set it before the recent swing high around the 1.2290 area, where selling pressure could step in.

Now, unlike the earlier examples where the MAEE formula is trading with the trend or in a range market, this is counter-trend trading, and I know that if I'm wrong, the market could reverse quickly against me. So for trade management, I'll trail my stop loss below the previous candle low. This means if the price breaks and closes below the previous day's low, I'll manually exit the trade even if it hasn't hit my target stop loss. This example highlights the flexibility of the MAEE formula. You can trade with the trend, in a range, or even against the trend.

Up next, I'll talk about when I stay out of the markets and why. Let's go.

Figure 8.7 – Trading example 7: stay out (USD/INR Daily)

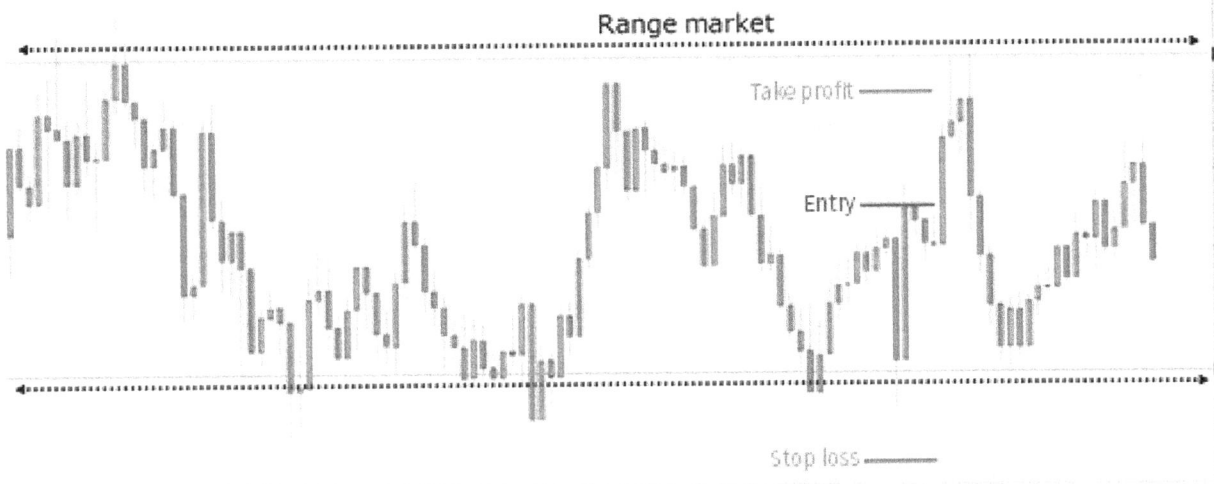

USDINR is in a range market. As you can see, the price re-tested support and reversed strongly back into the middle of the range. At this point, I have no interest in buying or selling. Why?

If you look at where the price is right now, it's in the middle of nowhere. If I were to go long at this level, my stop loss has to go 1 ATR below support (where my trade gets invalidated), and my target is around $72 just before resistance.

So if you were to calculate the risk-to-reward ratio, I'm risking $1.3 (entry at $71.4, stop loss at $70.1) to make $0.6 (target at $72)—not a trade I'm interested in making.

You might be thinking, "So Rayner, what's the minimum risk-to-reward ratio to aim for?" Recall that your risk to reward is only one part of the equation. The other is your winning rate. So if you have a high winning rate, you can get away with a risk-to-reward ratio of less than 1 to 1 (and vice versa). Personally, I want a minimum of 1 to 0.8 before the price hits the first "obstacle."

Figure 8.8 – Trading example 8: stay out (S&P500 Daily)

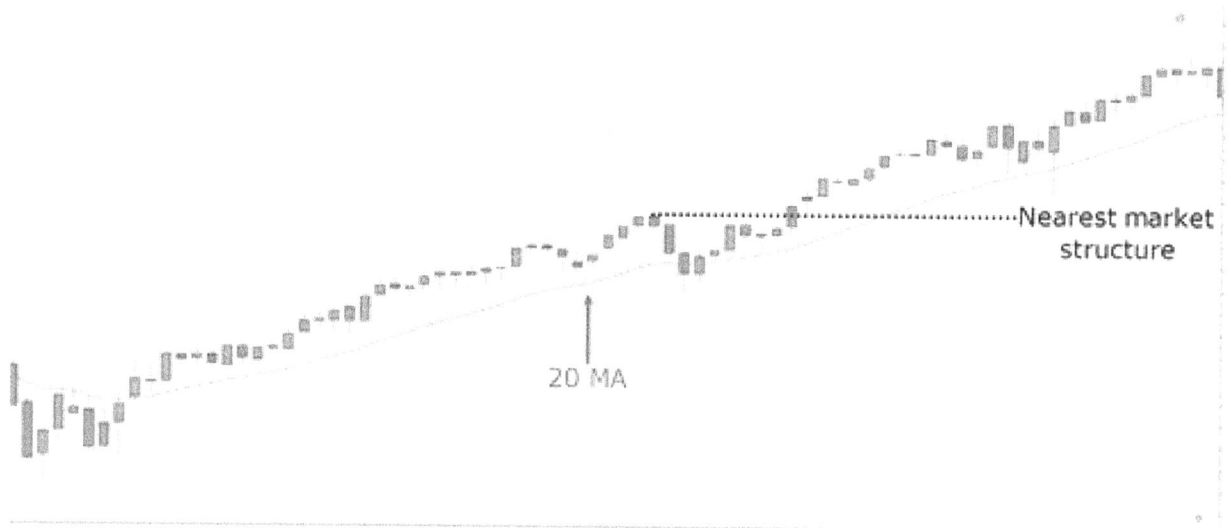

The S&P 500 is in a strong uptrend. One way to tell is to overlay it with the 20 MA because in a strong uptrend, the price will tend to stay above it for a sustained period. So why stay out of this market even though it's in an uptrend? There are two reasons:

23. The price is in no man's land. It's not near an area of value nor is there a buildup forming (so the MAEE and MBEE formula requirements have not been met).

24. Even if you were to buy, there's no logical place to set your stop loss since the nearest structure of the market is at $3150 (where previous resistance could become support).
So given these two factors, I'd rather stay out of the market.

My thought process here is based on the daily time frame. However, if you look at a lower time frame (for instance, the 15-minute time frame), there will be opportunities for you to trade because the market structure is different.

So the takeaway is this: Even if there are no trading opportunities in your time frame, it doesn't mean there are no opportunities for other participants because their time frames might be different.

Figure 8.9 – Trading example 9: stay out (T-Bond daily)

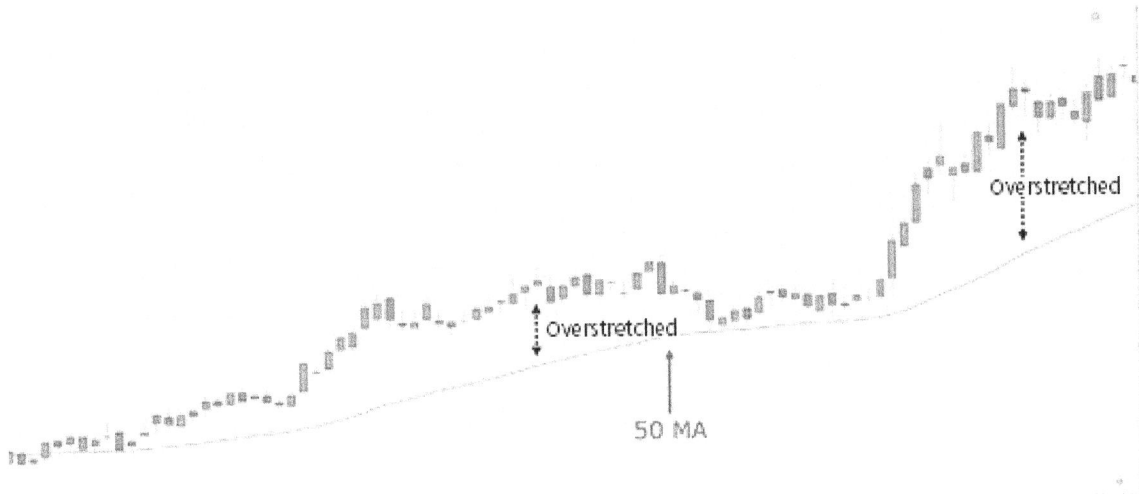

US T-Bond futures is in an uptrend, and if you were to classify this further, it's a healthy trend (because the price has "bounced off" multiple times). You might be thinking, "Why stay out of this market?" I'll explain.

1. As you can see, the price is "overextended" beyond the 50MA. If you were to buy right now, your stop loss would likely be triggered on the pullback if it isn't wide enough.

2. To set a proper stop loss, it has to go below the 50MA. This wide stop loss requires a smaller position size (if you want to keep your risk constant), which offers you a poor risk-to-reward ratio.

   The solution? Let the market come to you because it's better to trade near an area of value than to chase the breakout (and get stopped out on the pullback).

Figure 8.10 – Trading example 10: stay out (Gold Daily)

Gold is in an advancing stage after the price broke and closed above resistance. As you already know, just because the price is in an uptrend doesn't mean you should immediately buy. Why? Because there's no nearby price structure you can lean against to set your stop loss. So what now? You let the price come to you. Here are two possibilities for how this can play out:

1. The price re-tests the $1350 area (where previous resistance could become support) and forms a bullish price rejection. Then you can enter on the next candle's open and have your stop loss 1 ATR below support.

2. Alternatively, the price might not re-test previous resistance turned support. Instead, it might consolidate and form a buildup. Now, you don't want to jump the gun here and enter the breakout too early, so what you want to do is let the 20MA "catch up" with the lows of the buildup. When that happens, you can place a buy stop order above the highs of the buildup and go long on the breakout, and your stop loss can go 1 ATR below the lows of the buildup.

So yes, you're staying out of gold for now, but this doesn't mean you can go chill and watch Netflix. Instead, you must plan how the different scenarios could play out and how you could take advantage of these trading opportunities.

AT THIS POINT...

I've shared the thought process behind my trades with you. This includes my entries, exits, trade management—and most importantly, the why behind my decisions.

Although we're approaching the end of this book, that doesn't mean it's the end of your price action trading journey, because you're always a student of the markets. Don't forget that. And as you grow as a trader, you'll discover new trading strategies, techniques, and nuances that you can adopt for your own trading.